CULTURE SMART!

IRELAND

THE ESSENTIAL GUIDE TO CUSTOMS & CULTURE

ALEXANDRA FURBEE

KUPERARD

"The real voyage of discovery consists not in seeking new landscapes, but in having new eyes."

Adapted from Marcel Proust, *Remembrance of Things Past*

ISBN 978 1 78702 366 6

British Library Cataloguing in Publication Data
A CIP catalogue entry for this book is available
from the British Library

First published in Great Britain
by Kuperard, an imprint of Bravo Ltd
59 Hutton Grove, London N12 8DS
Tel: +44 (0) 20 8446 2440
www.culturesmart.co.uk
Inquiries: publicity@kuperard.co.uk

Design Bobby Birchall

The Culture Smart! series is continuing to expand.
All Culture Smart! guides are available as e-books, and many
as audio books. For further information and latest titles visit
www.culturesmart.co.uk

ALEXANDRA FURBEE, originally from Atlanta, Georgia, has lived in Ireland since 2014. She first moved to Dublin to pursue her graduate education—the lively culture, beautiful landscapes, and friendly people meant that she never left. Alexandra has a BA in Political Science from Flagler College, Florida, and an MA in Irish Studies from University College Dublin. She has worked in higher education administration in America and Ireland, and currently works at one of the largest universities in Dublin in Enrolment Planning and Research. In her free time, Alexandra loves to travel, read, and write for her blog *Candid Alexandra*.

CONTENTS

Set at the westernmost edge of Europe, facing the Atlantic, the beautiful island of Ireland has had an influence and endured a history out of all proportion to its size, and it has done so because of the people who live here. The Irish have given the world so much in the way of literature, music, and drama that it comes as no surprise that visitors have flocked here for generations to experience its distinctive culture and warm hospitality. In these pages we'll learn something about the ancient civilization and often turbulent history that have proved such fertile ground for Irish creativity.

There are many who venture here because they want to understand more about their own family background. In the USA nearly 10 percent of the population claim Irish ancestry, but perhaps the most famous American with Irish roots is President John F. Kennedy, whose great-grandparents were Irish immigrants who left for America in the mid-nineteenth century. It's a similar story in New Zealand, Canada, and Australia, where approximately 10 to 15 percent of the population of each country have Irish forebears. Among the far-flung Irish diaspora, collective memory is often shrouded in romantic myth and stereotypes that no longer apply.

Whatever their reason for coming, almost all visitors find that many of the assumptions they held about Ireland and the Irish fall apart rather quickly. In the last decade, the country has undergone a profound social, economic, and political transformation. After rebounding from the painful global financial crisis in 2008, Ireland saw an influx of multinational corporations in the technology and pharmaceutical sectors that gave the economy new momentum. Today it is a hub for tech innovation, and foreign investment is one of the economy's major drivers. In the political realm, the rise of new parties and coalitions are challenging the dominance of their traditional forerunners. In particular, the recent rise of Sinn Féin as a political force reveals a growing disillusionment with establishment politics on the part of young voters who desire real change. Across society, attitudes on issues such as LGBTQ rights and abortion have undergone shifts of tectonic proportions; an historic referendum in 2015 legalized same-sex marriage and a landmark vote in 2018 upended the ban on abortion in a momentous divergence from Ireland's conservative Catholic past. These are just two of many examples.

This book upacks all this and more so that you can understand the values and attitudes of the Irish today, as well as how they have been molded by their history and, indeed, their geography. It will acquaint you with their traditions, their rich musical and literary culture, how they like to let their hair down, and how they conduct business. This understanding will be appreciated by your hosts; it will open doors to you, and even open the hearts of a generous, talented people, justifiably proud of their unique identity. As the Irish say: *"Céad míle fáilte"*— One hundred thousand welcomes.

Ireland is a single geographical entity—an island off the western coast of Europe. It is home to two political units, one an independent self-governing republic, Eire (pronounced "AIR-uh"), often called "the Republic," to distinguish it from Northern Ireland, which is part of the United Kingdom with some elements of self-government.

Official Name	Eire, or Ireland	Article 4 of the Republic's 1937 constitution states "The name of the state is Eire or in the English language, Ireland."
Capital City	Dublin	
Main Cities	Dublin, Cork, Galway, Limerick	
Area	About 27,000 square miles (70,000 sq. km). Eire occupies 85% of the island of Ireland, all except the northeastern corner.	
Climate	Temperate	
Population	About 5.2 million. Well over a million in Dublin. Over 60% of the population live in urban areas, mostly within 50 miles (100 km) of Dublin. Growth rate: 1.12% per annum	
Currency	The Euro	
Ethnic Mix	77% Native Irish, 10.3% Other White (this includes UK- and EU-born nationals), 3.7% South Asian, small Jewish and Chinese minorities	
Family Size	1.3 children per family on average	
Language	Two official languages: Gaelic and English. Gaelic is studied in schools, but only a minority use it in daily life (they also speak English). Many Gaelic words appear in public life, however.	
Religion	About 70% officially Roman Catholic; 14.8% identify as athiest; 4% Protestant; around 2% Orthodox; small Islamic, Hindu, Sikh, and Buddhist communities	

Government	Parliament, called the *Oireachtas*, has two chambers: the Senate, *Seanad Eireann*, and the house of representatives, the *Dail Eireann*. The head of state is the President, elected for seven years. Real power lies with the *Taioseach*, or Prime Minister.
Local Government Structure	Eire is divided into 26 counties. Ancient Ireland was made up of four provinces, formerly kingdoms: Ulster, Munster, Leinster, and Connaught. Ulster is now mainly in Northern Ireland.
Legal System	The heads of the legal system are the judges of the Supreme Court, appointed by the President on the advice of the Prime Minister and cabinet. The legal system is based on English Common Law, but much modified by the Constitution and by laws and judgments made since independence.
Cost of Living	Currently the cost of living is much the same as in the United Kingdom.
Ports and Airports	Dublin and Cork are the main ports, Dublin and Shannon the main airports.
Media	*Raidió Teilifís Éireann*, the national broadcasting body, has two English television channels: RTE1 and Network 2, and an Irish-language channel TG4. The independent commercial station is TV3. BBC and other UK channels are available in much of the country as are Northern Irish transmissions. *Raidió Teilifís Éireann* has the five main radio channels: Radio 1 (Speech & Music), Radio 1 Extra (speech), 2FM (popular culture), Lyric FM (classical music), *Raidió na Gaeltachta* (Irish Language channel). There are 2 national commercial and numerous local radio stations.
English Media	Several large-circulation national newspapers including *The Irish Independent*, *The Irish Times*, *The Irish Examiner*

Electricity	The Irish electrical system operates on 220–240 volts, 50 Hz.	Sockets and plugs as in the UK. Visitors from continental Europe will need adapters. Americans will need adapters both for the voltage cycles and plugs and sockets.
Internet Domain	.ie	
Telephone	The international dialing code for Ireland is 00 353.	
Time	GMT Oct to Mar, plus 1 hr. in summer	

KEY FACTS: NORTHERN IRELAND

Official Name	Province of Northern Ireland	The Province is sometimes called Ulster, but actually includes only six of the original nine counties of the kingdom of Ulster.
Capital	Belfast	
Main Cities	Belfast, Londonderry, Omagh	
Area	5,500 square miles (14,000 sq. km)	
Climate	Temperate	
Population	1.9 million. Mostly in the east, where Belfast has a population of over 348,000.	
Currency	Pound Sterling. English notes and coins are legal tender, as are the notes issued by Scottish banks. Additionally four Northern Irish banks issue their own notes.	

Ethnic Mix	89% Northern Irish, many with Scottish forebears. Small Indian and larger Polish and Chinese communities
Family Size	Average number of children per woman: 2.0
Language	English
Religion	45.7% Catholic, 43.4% Protestant, the rest largely athiest
Government	Northern Ireland is part of the United Kingdom and elects 18 members to the British Parliament, but has its own Assembly at Stormont with limited legislative and administrative powers.
Legal System	As in the UK, with some modifications, notably under the Prevention of Terrorism Act 1974
Cost of Living	Lower than elsewhere in the UK
Media	Closely linked to those in the rest of the UK, and also overlaps with print, television, and radio in the Republic. Two publicly funded television channels, BBC1 and BBC2 with local content, as well as BBC4. The Commercial station is ITV Ulster. In addition digital channels are available from Eire and the rest of the UK. The five UK-wide BBC radio stations, as well as the three UK-wide commercial radio services (Classic FM, Talk Sport, and Virgin Radio) are also available. Two national radio stations: BBC Radio Ulster, operated by the BBC, and the commercial Downtown Radio, as well as several local radio stations.
Ports and Airports	Belfast is one of the UK's major ports. The international airport is about 20 miles from Belfast, but there is also a small single-runway airport within the city.
Electricity	240 volts, as in the rest of the UK
Telephone	The international code is 00 44, as in the UK.
Time	GMT Oct to Mar, plus 1 hr. in summer (BST)

CHAPTER ONE

LAND & PEOPLE

GEOGRAPHY AND CLIMATE

Ireland, commonly referred to as the "Emerald Isle," sits at the very edge of Europe, tethered a few miles off the coasts of Wales, England, and Scotland. Battered by the Atlantic but warmed by the Gulf Stream, Ireland has a temperate maritime climate resulting in mild winters and cooler summers. The climate can vary and change quickly, and the locals like to joke that you can experience all four seasons in a day. Ireland is the third-largest island in Europe. The landscape is made up of rolling hills, rugged coastlines, and countless lakes and rivers. The central part of the country contains plains and valleys while the west and northwest are covered in mountains.

Ireland's position and the nature of the land itself has shaped the way of life of the people and their attitudes toward themselves and others. For example, Ireland is famous for its verdant landscape, and this greenness has

A view of Twelve Pine Island against the backdrop of the Twelve Bens peaks in Connemara.

become part of the Irish national identity: the national flag is green, white, and orange; the sportsmen and women play in green; even the telephone boxes are green (or at least they were, when they were still in use).

Connemara on the west coast is untamed, captivated by the Twelve Bens (or Twelve Pins) mountain range. There are also several lakes, rivers, and dense green valleys. The shores are white sandy beaches, many of which are secluded, perfect for exploring, beachcombing, and swimming. Rocky cliffs and peaks overlook these beaches, making it a popular spot for walks. Connemara National Park provides several walking and hiking trails, one of the most well known leading to the summit of Diamond Hill, providing a sweeping view of the surrounding countryside.

The "Wishing Bridge" at the Gap of Dunloe, County Kerry.

In the northwest is Donegal, with magnificent beaches. Just south of Donegal is the town of Sligo which was immortalized by the poems of W. B. Yeats.

Ireland's elevations provide a unique and distinctive beauty. Slieve Donard, the highest peak of the Mourne Mountains, sweeps down to the sea from a height of just 2,790 feet (850 meters). Made famous by Irish songwriter Percy French, this sweeping range of grand peaks is an Area of Outstanding Beauty and a UNESCO Global Geopark. The Slieve Bloom Mountains, straddling the counties of Laois and Offaly, rise from the central plain of Ireland and are among some of the oldest mountains in Europe. Their central location also makes them easily accessible. The Wicklow Mountains in the east form the largest area of continuous high ground in Ireland. In

The port at Clidfen, County Galway.

southwestern county Kerry are the MacGillycuddy's Reeks, the highest mountains on the island, its tallest peak standing at 3,405 feet (1,038 meters).

Ireland is a country of hills and plains, but above all it is a land of rivers and lakes; the Republic alone has 537 square miles (1,390 square kms) of water. Most people have heard of the beautiful Lakes of Killarney, but few realize Lough Neagh in Ulster is the largest lake by surface area in the British Isles. Today, hydropower accounts for about 2.5 percent of the country's electricity generating capacity.

The "pleasant waters of the River Lee," the Blackwater, the Suir, the Nore, the Barrow, the Liffey, and the Lagan on which the city of Belfast stands, all flow toward the east. Only the Bann flows north; and the Shannon, 250 miles long (402 kms) and the longest river in the British Isles, flows south.

To the north of the Shannon lies the lovely county of Clare, with the unique landscape of the rocky Burren country. Galway, in its famous bay, is the major city of the west and looks to the sea rather than the land.

No rivers flow into the sea in Connacht, but there is no shortage of water. The west is often seen as the most distinctively Irish part of the country—it is certainly the wettest. The water-bearing clouds fresh from the Atlantic strike the rising ground and the rain comes down in bucketfuls. But there's still plenty left for the rest of the country.

The Emerald Isle's color derives from its climate, which involves a certain amount of rain. Even the driest parts around Dublin get around 128 days of rain a year, and an annual total of 29.5 inches (75 cm) of rainfall. New arrivals quickly learn never to leave home without an umbrella or waterproof gear, even in the sunniest months of May and June. Equally, it's best to be prepared for beautiful sunny days in February or November. The skies are often overcast, but the sun is always ready to surprise you by showing her face when she is least expected. The combination of sunshine and moisture makes for wonderful sunsets over Galway Bay and for glorious rainbows. And all you have to do is find the foot of a rainbow to claim a Leprechaun's crock of gold.

If an Irishman tells you it's "a fine soft day" he means it is refreshing; the air is crisp but not cold, just damp. The rain rarely turns to snow, and temperatures in the east range from about 39°F (4°C) in January to 68°F (20°C) in August.

The mild damp climate affects many aspects of Irish culture. In the midlands, peat moss fills former lakes and wetlands and over thousands of years has built up into raised peat bogs. Once dried, peat can be used for fuel, and so many bogs have been drained for this purpose. The scent of a peat fire (the Irish often call peat "turf") drifting from a cottage chimney is unforgettable. It's estimated that Ireland holds 60 percent of Europe's remaining active raised bogs.

Ireland is known for the excellence of its beef and dairy products and the majority of its agricultural output is made up of livestock and related products. Of around 140,000 farms in the country, almost 100,000 participate in some form of beef enterprise and this forms over 25 percent of the country's agricultural output. The main cereals grown in Ireland are wheat, oats, and barley, and these grains are used to feed animals and to make food such as bread and porridge. Even today, 84 percent of

Irish agricultural land is down to pasture or rough grazing. The green pastures of the central plain are devoted mainly to dairying, but also raise fine pigs, and the wonderful grass of the Curragh breeds famous horses. There are few golden fields of corn; instead, oats and potatoes are grown, and in the comparatively dry and sunny southeast, barley—Cork is famous for its brewing and distilling.

Off the west coast are the Aran Islands, positioned at the mouth of Galway Bay. These rocky places, battered by the seas and gales of the Atlantic, are famous for their lush landscapes, picturesque cottages, Aran sweaters, and its Irish-speaking inhabitants. By virtue of their relative isolation, the three islands—Inishmore, Inishmaan, and Inisheer—have maintained a traditional Irish life and in 2024 had a population of around 1,350.

Don't Overdo It!

Many visitors like to stock up on distinctive Irish clothing—Aran sweaters, tweeds, and the like. By all means wear them while in the country but be careful not to overdo it; a visitor who wears a lot of traditional clothing might find themselves the subject of a certain sly humor.

The islands have been inhabited for over four thousand years and are a treasure house of antiquities and Celtic remains. Though most islanders are fluent in English, Irish is still many people's first language, and there was a remarkably high level of Irish monolingualism until the end of the twentieth century. Eeking out a living against the elements, to catch fish islanders would brave the Atlantic rollers in *currachs*—frail canvas boats that they rowed with remarkable courage and skill.

Nowadays the island's economy is more prosperous. The islands attract around a quarter of a million visitors a year, most of them in the summer.

Northern Ireland, which comprises only about a fifth of the island, contains 27.1 percent of its population; most live in the east near Belfast, though it is easy to escape to areas of real peace.

The North's physical geography differs little from the rest of Ireland. You will sometimes hear the North called "Ulster," though this is not strictly correct—the old kingdom of Ulster also included three counties now in the Republic.

The weather is no less rainy than that of the Republic, and the winters are equally mild.

Northern Humor

Old Ulsterman: *If you can see Carrickfergus Castle on the opposite side of Belfast Lough that means it's going to rain.*
Visitor: *And if you can't see it?*
Old Ulsterman: *That means it's already raining.*

The damp climate and pure water were well suited to the cultivation and preparation of flax, and Northern Ireland was world famous for its linen.

Finally, Ireland is the best place to be on the planet if you want to avoid earthquakes. No epicenter has ever been found anywhere on the entire island!

IRISH SOCIETY AND PEOPLE

The pattern of life in Ireland has come to resemble that of much of the Western world. Superficially, it can be hard to tell an English, Scots, or Welsh person from someone from Ireland. People dress similarly, speak the same language, and have many of the same tastes. This was not always the case and underneath the surface, significant differences remain—many born of historical experience.

Ireland can be a complex place and its outward similarities can be misleading. To understand the people who call this island home, you must be aware of the events that have shaped, and continue to shape, their thoughts and feelings. Taking the time to learn about their customs, traditions, and the Irish way of doing things will be greatly appreciated by your hosts and do much to enrich your experience.

Ireland experienced centuries of English colonization and the catastrophic Great Famine in the nineteenth century led to considerable emigration and deaths. The English can be ignorant of Irish history—if they had made a better effort to understand it, things may have been different. Conversely, the Irish are steeped in their history, both real and mythical. Their history and their religion have forged the national consciousness—which is why, throughout this book, you will find plenty of snippets of history.

For nearly eight hundred years Ireland was colonized by the English. During much of that time, effective English government could only be imposed within 50 miles of Dublin, the so-called Pale of Dublin—those outside English control being considered barbarians and so, "beyond the Pale." But at other times English rule extended throughout the island and was often harsh, repressive, and bitterly resented.

An Open Society

The class structure in Ireland has evolved over centuries but has its foundations in English class hierarchies. The population was split into a distinct pecking order, the highest being landowners and Anglo-Irish aristocracy, followed by tenant farmers, laborers, and urban workers. The Anglo-Irish, once the landowning gentry, still exist, but are tolerated rather than revered—especially since Irish farmers are no longer tenants but own their land.

Once Ireland gained independence from Britain in the early twentieth century, a more egalitarian society was desired. Land distribution and agricultural reforms were attempted but historical discrimination in land ownership and traces of the old class system endured. This particularly occurred in rural areas where owning land still influenced social status. Ireland scarcely experienced the eighteenth and nineteenth century industrialization that created the working-class/middle-class division in English society, except to some extent in what is now Northern Ireland, and there the fiercely egalitarian nature of the dominant Presbyterian Church militated against obvious class differences.

The result is that Irish society is fairly heterogeneous, with most people having similar roots in rural culture. To suggest that there is absolutely no distinctive Irish urban working-class culture, however, is an exaggeration—as witnessed in the plays of Seán O'Casey and, more recently, the novels of Roddy Doyle. Another famous writer, Brendan Behan, was proud of being the working-class son of a Dublin painter and decorator. Yet his mother's family came from a family of farmers in County Meath, while his mother's brother, the poet Paedar Kearney, actually wrote the Irish national anthem, "The Soldiers' Song."

Nevertheless, given Dublin's size, a rural-urban divide is inevitable. Dublin in the new millennium was inundated with new money as successful entrepreneurs and entertainers paid lavish sums for the houses of the old English rulers. The term "Dublin 4," or "D4," actually refers to a postal area, but is used to sum up the cosmopolitan (some may say "entitled") attitudes of those who live there. Then there are the so-called "chattering classes"—intellectuals, politicians, bureaucrats, and professionals found in certain southside Dublin pubs. Country-dwellers can feel out of touch with city people, and can sometimes distrust them, though less so as advancements have made their way into the countryside. Class hierarchies in present day Ireland are multifaceted, shaped by elements such as education, income, and gentrification. Ireland has seen major economic success and increased standards of living since the late twentieth century, but inequality remains.

Status

Status can be derived either from wealth or talent, or like many other countries, who you know or what family you are born into.

The Irish revere their dead heroes, but toward the living they are likely to feel less reverential. Irish culture is naturally artistic, particularly in the arts of poetry, music, and drama, but those who excel in these fields are seen as part of society, less as some sort of elite.

Irish Irreverence

In England, the eminent poet Seamus Heaney (1939–2013) accepted the post of Professor of Poetry at Oxford University and was offered the title of Poet Laureate. As a republican, however, he refused. In Ireland he was respected and admired but not revered or put on a pedestal. Indeed, he was sometimes gently mocked as "Famous Seamus."

Tax Free Art

Income earned by writers, composers, visual artists, and sculptors from the sale of their work is exempt from tax in Ireland in certain circumstances, attracting talented artists from around the world. The work must be considered original and creative and have either cultural merit or artistic merit to qualify, and those that do are exempt from up to €50,000 in taxes. The presence of so many artists from around the world has been a major influence on society over the last quarter-century.

THE IMPORTANCE OF HISTORY
TO THE IRISH

It could be argued that there is no country in the world
where the attitudes and values of its modern inhabitants are
so much the product of their history. As we will see, certain
key events or concepts have become part of the Irish
mindset. You will hear people speaking of the "Island of
Saints and Scholars," or perhaps refer to the "Flight of the
Earls," "the Plantation of Ulster," the "Curse of Cromwell,"
"the Penal Laws," "the Protestant Ascendancy," "the 98,"
Robert Emmet's speech from the dock, or "The Liberator
Daniel O'Connell." Northern Protestants will talk about
"the Apprentice Boys of Derry" and "King Billy and the
Battle of the Boyne." And all spoken of as if they were
still living issues—as to many Irish people they are!

Island of Saints and Scholars

Ireland has been inhabited since about 7,900 BCE when
Mesolithic hunter-gathers arrived. Some four thousand
years later the Neolithic, or Stone Age, inhabitants arrived
by boat from Britain and constructed massive religious
monuments like the megalithic tomb at Newgrange (within
easy driving distance of Dublin and well worth a visit).

The sixth century BCE brought the Celts, and a
dynamic era of arts and crafts. Ireland rejoices in the
largest collection of prehistoric gold artifacts found in
Western Europe; you can see them at the National
Museum in Dublin.

Ireland is set apart from most of Europe by the fact that
it was never part of the Roman Empire, at a time when

Stone features on the megalithic tomb at Newgrange.

most of Europe had submitted to the Roman yoke. In fact, the Romans were not interested in occupying a country that had few metals of its own and could not grow the grain needed to feed their armies.

Greco-Roman classical learning and literacy came to Ireland with the introduction of Christianity and writing in the fifth century. Latin civilization fused with the Celtic decorative tradition to produce such masterpieces as the Ardagh Chalice, the Book of Durrow, and the Book of Kells.

Sometimes the monks grew bored with the slow, painstaking copying of the Gospels, and scribbled short lyrics in the margins of their work, like this, written in an eighth-century copy of St. Paul's Epistles.

I and Pangur Ban, my cat,
'Tis a like task we are at;
Hunting mice is his delight,
Hunting words I sit all night . . .

Better far than praise of men
'Tis to sit with book and pen . . .

(Extract from *Pangur Ban*, trans. Robin Flower)

Among the hundreds of monasteries founded at this time were the great centers of Clonmacnoise in County Offaly, and Monastarboice in County Louth. This was a golden age for Ireland, which became a refuge for classical scholarship and Christian learning in a Europe that was elsewhere sinking back into barbarity. Hence the pride in being the "Island of Saints and Scholars!"

Ornately carved Celtic cross at the ancient monestary site of Clonmacnoise.

The Vikings and St. Brendan

The Viking invasions from the ninth century onward
brought death and destruction but also trade, currency,
and the foundation of most of the major towns including
Dublin. It was in the ninth century that *The Voyage of
St. Brendan* was written, which tells the story of an abbot
from three centuries prior voyaging across the sea in
search of a heavenly land promised by God to the saints.

Tara and the High Kings

All this time, Ireland was divided into separate
kingdoms. There were "High Kings" (*Ardrí na hÉireann*
in Irish) based at the Hill of Tara in County Meath, with
a great hall 700 feet (240 meters) long, but their title was
honorary and sacred, and they wielded no real power
over other rulers. While all old Irish roads lead to the
Hill of Tara, its importance is purely symbolic and all
that now remains are earthworks. Yet these various
kingdoms shared a language, a set of laws—the Brehon
Laws—and a common artistic, literary, and musical
culture when as early as the third century CE the High
King, Cormac, founded what was in effect a royal
academy to promote poetry and the law.

In 1014 the High King Brian Boru defeated the
Norsemen at the Battle of Clontarf—typically he was
also fighting other Irishmen, the men of Leinster having
sided with the Vikings!

The Normans

An Anglo-Norman adventurer, the Earl of Pembroke,
known as Strongbow, arrived in 1170, invited across

by an Irish king who was quarreling with the High King. The mounted and mailed Norman knights with their big horses, lances, archers (the Irish only had slings), and impregnable castles were in a different class from the *kernes*, the Irish foot soldiers. They soon controlled all of Ireland except for part of Ulster, and for the first time Ireland was theoretically part of the kingdom of England.

Very little of the island actually came under direct English rule. Most of the local Norman and native Irish chiefs were a law unto themselves, and the King of England's writ did not run beyond the Pale, some 50 miles round Dublin.

The impact of the Normans is complicated. While they substantially influenced Irish society in areas such as architecture, culture, and law, their occupancy added to centuries of opposition and hostility between the Norman colonizers and the Irish people.

More Irish than the Irish!

The Norman barons intermarried with the Irish, adopted Irish ways and laws, and even learned to speak Irish, so that Norman surnames like Fitzgerald, Costello, or Butler, now seem as Irish as O'Connor or O'Brian. Indeed, the Norman lords were accused of being *Hibernicis ipsis Hibernior*— "More Irish than the Irish." Even today the visitor who overzealously adopts Irish ways may be jokingly referred to as "More Irish than the Irish."

The Flight of the Earls and the Plantation of Ulster

Only in the late Tudor era and the sixteenth century was Ireland beyond the Pale brought anything like under control. This century also saw the start of the great religious divide between Protestants and Catholics, since the introduction of the Elizabethan prayer book was the first serious attempt to impose the Protestant Reformation on the Irish people. In Tudor times Ulster in the North was the heartland of the native Irish. Its great chieftain, Hugh O'Neill, Earl of Tyrone, was brought up in Queen Elizabeth's court. Yet when England was at war with Spain, he and his powerful neighbor, Hugh O'Donnell, marched their men all the way to the south to try to rescue a Spanish force besieged in Kinsale. They were routed.

O'Neill was pardoned in 1603 but hated to serve where he had formerly ruled. In 1607 he and the Earl of Tyrconnell, Hugh O'Donnell's son, fled to France and then Rome. Their exit left a void in leadership among the Irish nobility which the English Crown exploited and the "Flight of the Earls" was followed by the dispossession of many Catholics in Ulster, their lands given to Englishmen and, especially, Scots—the two realms having just been united under James I of England (and VI of Scotland).

These colonists would be hated by the Irish Catholics they displaced and would support the Crown. This was the "Plantation of Ulster," and it had profound and enduring consequences on the demographic and religious composition of Northern Ireland. It explains why so many people in Ulster have Scottish names, are Presbyterians, and remain loyal to the British Crown.

The Curse of Cromwell

In 1641, just before the English Civil War, the Irish rebelled and the question of who should control the forces sent against them actually precipitated the war. During the war they theoretically sided with the King, Charles I, and after the King was defeated and executed, they were savagely suppressed by the leader of the Parliamentary army in Ireland: Oliver Cromwell. The massacres following the sieges of Drogheda and Wexford in 1649 and his seizure of great swathes of his Irish opponents' lands have made Cromwell a name loathed in the South: to put the "Curse of Cromwell" on someone is a terrible imprecation.

Cromwell's bloody campaign resulted in the displacement of Irish landowners, their land in turn given to English soldiers and colonists. The campaign also saw a deterioration in the authority of Irish Catholic nobility and increased prejudice against Catholics with the introduction of severe penal laws that restricted their rights.

King Billy, the Apprentice Boys, and the Battle of the Boyne

When the exiled Charles II returned to England to accept the throne in 1660, many Irishmen hoped to get their lands back. But Charles was only restored at the invitation of Parliament and could do nothing. In 1685 Charles's brother James, a Catholic, became King. James II made himself so unpopular that William of Orange, the Protestant Dutch ruler (married to James's sister Mary), was invited to take over the English throne.

King William III at the Battle of the Boyne, by eighteenth century painter Jan Wick.

James turned to Ireland, where in 1689 he attempted to stage a comeback and was welcomed by the Catholic population. James was denied command of the City of Londonderry, however, when thirteen Protestant apprentice boys seized the keys and shut the gates in his face. The subsequent Siege of Derry left thirty thousand Protestants besieged in the city for 105 days, holding out until an English relief force belatedly arrived. When called on to give in, they replied "No Surrender," and this phrase has been the watchword of the Northern Irish Protestants ever since.

To this day Protestant Loyalists still prefer to trust to themselves rather than the English, and a fraternal society named The Apprentice Boys of Derry was founded in 1814 and until today remains committed to maintaining and celebrating the spirit of the so-called Defenders of Londonderry.

On July 12, 1690, William of Orange, riding a white horse, defeated the Catholic Irish under James at the

Battle of the Boyne. King Billy and his white horse
are still to be seen painted on the side of many Belfast
end-of-terrace houses, together with the words "1690
No Surrender!"

James fled to Dublin, where he complained that the
Irish (who actually fought very hard) had run away. A lady
present remarked "Your Majesty won the race!" James II
is not a popular figure in Irish history and it would be as
well not to translate his nickname, Seamus a Chaca. It is
not unconnected with what flows through sewers!

The battle had considerable repercussions for Ireland's
political and religious circumstances, as it solidified
Protestant authority over the country and is still
commemorated by the Orange Order, a Protestant fraternal
organization in Northern Ireland today. The "Twelfth of
July" celebrates the victory at the Boyne and is known for
the parades and bonfires within Protestant communities.
Needless the say, the event is recalled rather differently
by Catholics.

The Penal Laws

The Protestant victory led to the enactment of the
"Penal Laws" against Catholics in 1695. These were a
series of prejudicial laws enacted by the Irish Parliament
that sanctioned several constraints on Catholics, such
as bans around observing their religion, owning land,
and receiving an education. The laws had serious
social, economic, and political repercussions, causing
severe poverty, disenfranchisement, and ultimately the
deterioration of traditional cultural and religious practices.
Many landowners converted to the Anglican Church of

Ireland as a means of avoiding the restrictions. By 1778, when the penal laws began to be repealed, only 5 percent of the land was Catholic owned.

The Protestant Ascendancy

The eighteenth century, known as the age of the "Protestant Ascendancy," saw the Protestant minority acquire political, economic, and social supremacy over the Catholic majority. Following the enactment of the Penal Laws, Protestant landowners owned a disproportionate supply of land relative to their numbers and regulated much of Ireland's resources. The Irish Parliament, from which Catholics were excluded, had considerable authority. It was during this time many of Ireland's great houses were built. Dublin acquired its beautiful redbrick Georgian squares, and the city became a fashionable center.

The rise of Irish nationalism in the nineteenth century challenged Protestant hegemony.

The United Irishmen and the '98

The rise of Irish nationalism in the nineteenth century challenged Protestant hegemony. Inspired by the American and French Revolutions, the mainly Protestant "United Irishmen," led by Wolfe Tone and Lord Edward Fitzgerald, sought to secure "equal representation of all the people" in a national government that would unite Irish Catholics and Protestants with a vision of a shared future.

In 1796 a French fleet of thirty-five ships crammed with thousands of troops fresh from victories all over Europe anchored off Bantry Bay and were ready to come to the aid of the rebels, but a week of fierce gales made it impossible for them to land and they sailed away. The English soldiers' cruel floggings of anyone they thought might reveal information about the United Irishmen were largely responsible for the rising known as "the '98 Rebellion" two years later. But no well-armed French professionals arrived to take on the British. Instead, the Irish had to make do with traditional weapons—homemade pikes manufactured by the local blacksmiths. The '98, as it is otherwise known, spread to different parts of the country, but following a few minor successes, the rebels were crushed at the battle of Vinegar Hill outside Wexford. In the North, the Presbyterians, who also suffered under the Penal Laws, actively supported the rebellion, but to no avail. The response from the British was severe and was marked by extensive violence and oppression. Thousands of rebels died in battle or were executed, and martial law was enforced in many areas.

The failed rebellion led to the passing of the Act of Union 1800, which joined the Kingdom of Ireland with the Kingdom of Great Britain, creating the United Kingdom of Great Britain and Ireland, and saw the end of the Irish Parliament. (The old Irish Parliament building in Dublin today houses the Bank of Ireland.)

Robert Emmet led an abortive rising in Dublin in 1803, which proved a fiasco, but his speech from the dock when he was condemned to death has rung down the years.

Let no man write my epitaph. When my country takes her place among the nations of the earth, then and not till then let my epitaph be written.

The Liberator

Daniel O'Connell, born into one of the few remaining families of prosperous Catholic landowners, is still known as "the Liberator." He held mass meetings—one at Tara, numbered nearly a million people—and pressured the British government into eventually granting basic civil rights and full Catholic emancipation in 1829. Irish Catholics could now sit in Parliament at Westminster, Catholic bishops and archbishops were accepted, and many Catholic churches were built. O'Connell also endorsed the repeal of the Act of Union, intending to reinstate an independent Irish legislature. Although his attempts to accomplish the repeal were not successful, his legacy and campaigning strengthened the continuing ambition for Irish independence.

THE MAKING OF MODERN IRELAND

The Great Famine and Emigration

A series of events since 1845 have had a colossal significance in defining not just the political and economic structure of modern Ireland but also its culture. These key events are the Great Famine and Emigration, Evictions and the Land Acts, the Gaelic Revival, the Easter Rising and the "Tan War," Irish War of Independence, the Anglo-Irish Treaty of 1921, and the Irish Civil War.

Although Ireland is much farther from America than it is from Britain, since the mid-nineteenth century there has been a great sense of kinship between the Americans and the Irish. When John F. Kennedy was elected

President, many Irish people saw him as "their" president. Galway even renamed its main square "John F. Kennedy Memorial Park."

The key occurrence in this orientation toward America was the Great Hunger of the 1840s.

The Great Famine was a disastrous time in Ireland's history that occurred between 1845–1852. It was a time of tremendous hardship, death, and extensive emigration, leaving a long-lasting impact on Ireland and its people. Folk memories of those terrible times are an important facet of the Irish psyche.

The collapse of the potato crop was the principal cause of the Famine. The potato blight, caused by the fungus *Phytophthora infestans,* ravaged potato crops all over the country, and a substantial portion of the population were tenant farmers who were heavily reliant on potatoes as their main supply of food which were nutritious and easy to grow.

Ireland was ruled by Britain at this time, and British policies exacerbated the famine. There were widespread deaths from starvation and from typhus, known as "famine fever." Agricultural products such as grains, vegetables, and meats were still being exported to Britain throughout the famine, increasing the agony of the Irish people, and led to a terrible sense of betrayal.

I ventured through the parish this day to ascertain the condition of the inhabitants and although a man not easily moved, I confess myself unmanned by the extent and density of suffering I witnessed, more especially among the women and little children,

> *crowds of whom were seen scattered over the turnip*
> *fields, like a flock of famished crows devouring the*
> *raw turnips, and mostly half naked, shivering in the*
> *snow and sleet, uttering exclamations of despair,*
> *while their children were screaming with hunger.*
> *I am a match for anything else I may meet here,*
> *but this I cannot stand.*
>
> (Captain Wynne, Inspecting Officer,
> West Clare, 1846)

The "Great Hunger" sowed in Irish hearts a profound bitterness toward the English. It is one of the most defining events of Ireland's history.

By contrast, huge gratitude was felt toward the people and government of the United States for taking in so many who fled.

> *What captivity was to the Jews, exile has been to*
> *the Irish. America and American influence has*
> *educated them.*
>
> (Oscar Wilde, 1889)

The Irish population in 1840 was 6.5 million. It's estimated that the Famine caused about 1 million deaths between 1845 and 1851 either from starvation or hunger-related disease. A further 1 million Irish people emigrated to mainly America, Australia, New Zealand, or Canada. It was many years before the Irish population got back to half of what it had been in 1840. It was only in 2022 that the population of the Republic of Ireland surpassed 5 million for the first time since the 1851 Census.

The Irish Have Long Memories

Despite the length of time that has passed, the Great Famine has not been forgotten and maintains a central position in the country's cultural memory. In 1994, the much-loved singer-songwriter Sinéad O'Connor had a national hit with a song simply entitled "Famine." In 2020, Irish public broadcaster Raidió Teilifís Éireann (RTÉ) marked the 175th anniversary of the Great Hunger with a two-part documentary that explored the origins, development, and legacy of the catastrophe.

Soon after the Famine a new word entered the vocabulary of Rebellion: "Fenian." The name comes from *Fianna Éireann*, the legendary band of Irish warriors led by the fictional Finn MacCool. Fenian were members of an Irish nationalist secret society that was most active in Ireland, the United States, and Britain, particularly in the 1860s, and pledged to wage guerrilla war against the British.

The father of the modern submarine, John Philip Holland (1841–1914), was a former member of the Catholic teaching order, the Christian Brothers. After the US Navy determined his submarine designs as unworkable, the Fenians funded Holland's research and development, and in 1881, "the Fenian Ram" was launched in the hope that it would prove to be the answer to Britain's naval supremacy. But the Irish cause was to make its greatest gains in this period by political, rather than by military action.

The Home Rule Movement

The Home Rule movement was one that campaigned for Irish self-government within the United Kingdom of

Great Britain and Ireland. It was the predominant political movement of Irish nationalism from 1870 to the end of the First World War. Toward the end of the nineteenth century Charles Stewart Parnell, leader of the Irish Parliamentary Party in the British House of Commons, dominated Irish politics. His aim was for Ireland to achieve self-governance, but with Ireland remaining subject to Queen Victoria. Parnell's eighty-five Irish Party seats were critical since they held the balance between the two main parties, the Conservatives and Liberals, and he was assisted by the fact that Minister William E. Gladstone, the Liberal leader, sympathized with his views.

Parnell fought savagely against absentee Irish landlords living in England who were evicting their tenants to consolidate their Irish lands into more viable and profitable units. It was Parnell who suggested in a

speech in 1880 that those responsible for carrying out the actual evictions should be ostracized. "You must show what you think of him … by isolating him from the rest of his kind as if he were a leper of old, you must show him your detestation of the crime he has committed."

Charles Stewart Parnell.

Boycotting

In so doing Parnell introduced a new word into the English language. The first victim of this treatment was Charles Cunningham Boycott, who was a British land agent. Ever since the word "boycott" has been used for this sort of action.

Parnell fell from office when it was revealed that he was having an affair with a married woman, an event that alienated him from his Catholic following. He was deposed in December 1890 and was dead within the year.

Gladstone proposed several Home Rule bills that were defeated in the House of Lords, but he and his party had more success with laws that enabled tenants to buy their own land. The state bought out the landlords and advanced mortgages to the former tenants that worked out to be a lot less than they had been paying as rent. Further "Land Purchase Acts" in 1903 and 1909 led to the principle of compulsory sale by the landlords, so that even before Independence the Catholic former tenants already owned the greater part of the agricultural land in Ireland.

The Irish Love of the Land

The Land Acts were a series of legislative measures enacted in the late nineteenth and early twentieth centuries and explain why Irish agriculture takes the form of thousands of small farms, rather than large tracts as in America or even Britain. The new laws endeavored to tackle the extreme social and economic issues caused by land ownership and tenant-landlord relations in Ireland, diminishing the power of landlords and expanding land-ownership by tenants. Today the average holding is still only 32 hectares. Irish farmers are fiercely attached to their land, which for so many years was owned by others.

Independence and Partition

By the late nineteenth and early twentieth centuries, demand for Irish independence was increasing, driven by a longing for political and cultural autonomy. The 1916 Easter Rising was the catalyst for the fight for independence. Irish republicans staged a rebellion against British rule in Dublin. Although the Rising was quickly repressed, it ultimately increased support for the Irish cause. After the Rising, Irish republicans came together under Sinn Féin (pronounced "shin-FAYN," meaning "We Ourselves"), and at the 1917 *ard fheis* ("High Assembly") the party committed itself for the first time to the formation of an Irish Republic. In 1918, Sinn Féin won the majority of Irish seats in the general election and instituted the First Dáil Éireann.

Shortly afterward, the War of Independence broke out in 1919, where the Irish Republican Army (IRA) employed guerrilla warfare against British services. The IRA, under the legendary leadership of Michael Collins, fought against the British Auxiliary Forces, ex-servicemen known as the "Black and Tans" from the color of their rather makeshift uniforms. Many acts of brutality occurred in the "Tan War" and the British Auxiliary Forces sometimes behaved more like terrorists than disciplined troops. This struggle led to the Anglo–Irish Treaty in 1921, whereby twenty-six of the thirty-two counties were granted the status of a "Free

State," which afforded them the same constitutional status as other countries within the British Commonwealth. But the Treaty led to division among Irish republicans, with a substantial amount against it as they remained subservient to Britain in various important matters and viewed it as a betrayal to the Easter Rising of 1916 which declared an Irish Republic. The refusal of many Irishmen to accept these limitations led to the Civil War of 1922–1923.

Perhaps the most controversial aspect of the Anglo-Irish Treaty was the provision that allowed for Northern Ireland to not form part of the Irish Free State. This subsequently resulted in the partition of Ireland, with Northern Ireland remaining a part of the United Kingdom and separate from the rest of Ireland that became the Irish Free State (and later, in 1949, the "Republic of Ireland"). The border created as a result of partition was to become a source of conflict for decades.

The Origin of the Main Irish Political Parties

Disagreements over the Anglo-Irish Treaty eventually caused the split of Fianna Fáil from Sinn Féin in 1926. Those who were prepared to accept the Treaty, however, ultimately became Fine Gael (1933). They won the civil war but at the cost of the assassination of Michael Collins. Fianna Fáil and Fine Gael later became the two main political parties in the Irish Parliament.

Sinn Féin advanced during The Troubles, placing significance on Irish reunification and progressive social policies. The Labor Party (1912), rooted in the trade union movement, focused on workers' rights and social justice.

The Orange Order and the Twelfth of July

Every July 12 you will see men parading through the
cities of Northern Ireland on the anniversary of the
Battle of the Boyne. They wear traditional Orange
regalia, including orange sashes, bowler hats, and white
gloves, and sometimes break into a curious shuffling
dance step known as the "Orange Shuffle." They are
accompanied by marching bands—silver bands and
brass bands, but especially fife and drum bands. They
are members of "the Orange Order," a society founded
in 1795 dedicated to defending the Protestant religion.

The Twelfth of July and Orange Order parades have
long been a source of debate in Northern Ireland. The
routes of the parades at times either pass through or
beside predominantly Catholic and Irish nationalist
neighborhoods, leading to conflict and sometimes
even violence. Today they are a reflection of continuing
sectarian divisions.

With the outbreak of the First World War, the Ulster
Volunteers patriotically enlisted in the British Army.
It was in gratitude for the "blood sacrifice" of these
volunteers (who were killed almost to a man in the Battle
of the Somme) that six of the nine counties of Ulster
were separated from the rest of Ireland to remain part of
the United Kingdom. We are still living with the results
of this division over a hundred years later.

Ireland became a republic in all but name after Fianna
Fáil, led by Eamon De Valera, came to power in 1932,
and especially after his new constitution of 1937. Ireland
was neutral in the Second World War, and following
the Republic of Ireland Act 1948, the UK parliament

passed the Ireland Act 1949 that officially declared Ireland a republic, allowing them to leave the British Commonwealth.

Throughout the early years of independence, the Irish government maintained a highly protectionist economy. The country remained fairly insular: peaceful, charming, but with a markedly lower standard of living than its neighbors and an economy still dominated by the British market.

To add to Ireland's difficulties, De Valera refused to continue repaying the British government loans that had enabled farmers to buy their land. The result was the Anglo-Irish trade war (also called the Economic War) that lasted six years and did nothing to improve the Irish economy or North/South relations, except perhaps between the thousands of smugglers on either side of the border.

The new constitution of 1937 (personally supervised by De Valera) outlawed both contraception and divorce and implied—nicely, but categorically—that a woman's place was in the home. Whereas elsewhere in Europe the number of women in work was constantly increasing, in Ireland the figure decreased.

Eager for a better life, many emigrated abroad. Some half a million people, a number equivalent to 80 percent of people born in the Free State between 1931 and 1941, left during this period. It was a level of emigration unseen since the Great Hunger of the 1840s.

America and Australia remained the preferred destinations, but the chances of returning were small. Like those who went before them, many young Irishmen left the countryside to earn better money in England in the building trade. Most of them intended to make enough money to return to Ireland and marry, but all too many never did.

All this has changed drastically in the last seventy years. Ireland today is vastly different from what it was in the 1950s. And it's the Ireland of today that the following pages of this book explores.

THE MAIN CITIES

Ireland's cities are enchanting and its towns each often benefit from having their own character that distinguishes them from their neighbors. Visitors will be happy to know that Irish cities are usually quite compact, so those in a hurry will find they can cover a lot of ground in a relatively short space of time. Wherever you will be, the countryside will never be very far. Even in Belfast, a typical industrial conurbation, you have only to look upward to see the empty hills that surround three sides of the city. And in Dublin, the largest of the Irish cities, you can catch glimpses of the nearby mountains. Take a short drive out of the city and you can find yourself in unspoiled country.

Dublin

Dublin—the national capital and the capital of Leinster province—has a history that can be traced back over a thousand years. Its name comes from the Irish word Duibhlinn, "*dubh*" meaning black or dark,

Mellows Bridge over River Liffey, Dublin.

and "*linn*" meaning pool, referring to a dark tidal pool where the River Piddle met the River Liffey to form a deep pool at Dublin Castle. The name of the city in modern Irish is Baile Átha Cliath ("BOLL-yah AW-hah CLEE-ah") and means "town of the hurdled ford." In 2024 the city was home to approximately 1.2 million inhabitants.

Despite municipal vandalism in the 1960s and 1970s, Dublin is still—at least in part—a town of lovely Georgian squares and of open spaces. Phoenix Park is the largest walled park in Europe, and herds of deer roam in it.

Dublin's cultural scene is bursting with an abundance of museums, theaters, and festivals. Events such as Bloomsday (commemorating *Ulysses* by James Joyce), the Dublin International Film Festival, and the Bram Stoker Festival attract visitors from around the country and world. The National Museum of Ireland, The Little Museum of Dublin, and The Gaiety Theatre are all Dublin-based, as is the National Art Gallery. There are four universities in the capital: Trinity College Dublin (home to one of Ireland's great national treasures, the eighth-century Book of Kells, said to be the most beautiful book in the world), University College Dublin, Dublin City University, and Technological University Dublin.

The city's top exports are pharmaceuticals, organic chemicals, and optical medical devices and are heavily exported to the United States, Germany, and the United Kingdom. In recent decades, Dublin has also become a vibrant tech and financial services hub and houses offices of many large multinational companies.

Cork

Ireland's second largest city, Cork, is located in the southwest of the country. It is reputedly the friendliest city in Ireland and its citizens the most talkative in a generally garrulous country. Known as the "Rebel County" due to its record of opposition against British rule, Cork and its citizens played a powerful role in the Irish War of Independence and the Irish Civil War.

Cork City is on the River Lee; its streets are built over waterways where ships would have been anchored. As in Dublin, the Danes were formative in the city's initial development. Vikings set up a trading settlement in the ninth century known as "Corcach," (meaning marsh) that ultimately evolved into what we now know as Cork.

Cork City is home to several pharmaceutical companies including Johnson & Johnson, Pfizer, and Novartis. Possibly the most famous product to come from the Cork pharmaceutical industry is Viagra. Cork is also currently the European headquarters of Apple, and over three thousand people are employed in manufacturing, research and development, and customer support.

Outside of its working life, Cork is well known for its gin, its whiskey, for Beamish stout, and for Father Matthew. When Cork people talk of "the Statue," they mean that of Father Theobald Matthew (his name is spelled "Mathew" on its plinth). Father Matthew founded the Catholic temperance movement that became the Pioneers. The success of the Pioneers is one of several reasons why the image of the drunken Irish is far from true of most Irish people, especially those in the countryside.

The city's port, called Cobh, has Ireland's only dedicated cruise terminal—in the past it was the departure point for millions of Irish people who emigrated to North America.

A view of the harbor at Cobh, County Cork.

Just outside the city's borders is the popular Blarney Castle, where tourists lean backward and nearly break their necks in order to kiss an unhygienic bit of rock called the blarney stone in the belief that it will give them the gift of the gab. If you don't fancy risking life and limb, the gardens and historic features are also worthwhile destinations.

Galway

On the west coast sits the charismatic city called Galway, the capital of bleakly beautiful Connacht. It is a wonderfully lively city with many young people, most of them students, who make up 20 percent of its roughly eighty-six thousand inhabitants. It's full of musical pubs and lively markets, is a center for the Irish language, and is the gateway to picturesque Connemara and the Aran Islands. The medieval history of the city is clear in its architecture, including the Spanish Arch and Lynch's Castle. The Galway Races and the Galway International Arts Festival also always draw large crowds.

Limerick

In the mid-west of Ireland lies Limerick, a city with a blend of contemporary and historical elements.

Best explored on foot, the city has a buzzing cultural life as well as riverside cafes and bars situated on the Shannon estuary and steeped in history. King John's Castle, Saint Mary's Cathedral, and Thomond Park should be on every visitor's sightseeing list. The city's university (UL) adds a bustling student culture.

Belfast

Belfast is the capital of Northern Ireland, though it still holds substantial cultural and historical ties with Ireland. Its population is about three hundred fifty thousand but over six hundred thousand live within 10 miles of the city.

Belfast's status as a major city began in the eighteenth century with the Industrial Revolution. The city's harbor and its closeness to natural coal and iron stores supported the development of shipbuilding, linen manufacturing, and engineering industries. Belfast's Harland and Wolff shipyard notably produced the RMS Titanic.

Over the last several decades Belfast has undergone a far-reaching transformation that has seen it shift into a dynamic cultural center with a flourishing literary and art scene. Landmarks such as Titanic Belfast, Crumlin Road Gaol, and Belfast City Hall have also seen the city emerge as a tourist destination. Belfast has been able to move past its difficult history—terrible air raids during the war followed by the damaging effects of The Troubles from 1969 which led to a drop in population—and establish itself as a creative and forward-looking city.

Londonderry

Londonderry—or "Derry" to its mainly Catholic population—is the second-largest city in Northern Ireland. The city's walls that date back to the seventeenth century are well preserved and surround the town center. The city's architecture is a blend of medieval, Georgian, and Victorian styles that highlight its diverse heritage.

Derry played a pivotal role in the history of Northern Ireland, especially during The Troubles. Derry's substantial Catholic nationalist population endured a history of discrimination in areas such as housing and employment. One of the most well-known events in Derry at this time was Bloody Sunday (January 30, 1972) when British troops killed thirteen unarmed protestors who were taking part in a civil rights march. Today, Derry has made tremendous advances to rectify the city's divided past and to promote reconciliation. The Peace Bridge, a cycle and pedestrian bridge, connects the two sides of the River Foyle, representing the city's aspiration for unity.

Whether a person refers to the city as "Derry" or "Londonderry" will often depend on their political or cultural affiliation. Nationalists and Catholics frequently use "Derry," emphasizing the city's Irish heritage and cultural identity, while Unionists and Protestants typically use "Londonderry," accentuating the city's historical ties to London and British rule.

POLITICS IN THE REPUBLIC

Ireland is a parliamentary democracy with a written constitution and a two-chamber parliament, the *Oireachtas* (pronounced "ERR-UHK-THUHS"), which consists of the President of Ireland, and the two houses of Dáil Éireann and Seanad Éireann. The senate, *Seanad Éireann* ("SHAN-ud-AIR-IN") has a total of sixty members, six elected by the Universities, forty-three from vocational panels, and eleven nominated by the *Taoiseach* ("TEE-shock"), the prime minister. The principal chamber is the *Dail Éireann* ("DOYL-AIR-UHN"), the House of

Representatives, whose 160 members are elected by a complex form of proportional representation.

By law, a general election must be held at least once every five years. Fundamental changes have to be approved by referendum: divorce (accepted 1995), abortion (rejected 2002), and same-sex marriage (accepted 2015) being a few notable examples. The president, who is directly elected every seven years, does not exercise an executive role. However, supreme command of the defense forces is vested in the president who also receives and credits ambassadors and carries out ceremonial duties. Real power lies with the Taoiseach (formally appointed by the president), who sits in the Dail as an elected member.

Criticizing politicians is a popular Irish pastime, but the complexity of the Irish political system with its many nuances is beyond most outsiders.

The Garda

The Republic's police force, *An Garda Síochána* ("Garda shi-ckhana"), often called "the Guards," are unarmed. They are well integrated into the community, and visitors should not hesitate to call on their services.

Up to the 1980s, the civil war that followed independence in 1922 formed a basic dividing line in the Irish political system, though the oldest political party in Ireland is the Labor Party, dating back to the time of James Larkin, the Trade Union leader.

Back in 1990 the election of a liberal woman, Mary Robinson, as President was such a success that another woman, Mary McAleese, succeeded her. This shift away from old stereotypes was also marked by an amendment to Articles 2 and 3 of the Irish Constitution, which claimed Northern Ireland as part of a United Ireland. As amended, they grant the right to be "part of the Irish Nation" to all those people born on the island of Ireland; the articles also express a desire for the peaceful political unification of the island subject to the consent of the people of Northern Ireland and Ireland. Equally remarkably, in 2011, the late Queen Elizabeth became the first British monarch to visit the Republic, where she and the President made speeches of reconciliation and friendship.

POLITICS IN NORTHERN IRELAND

For years "The Troubles" in the North plagued all of Ireland. The Troubles began in 1969, and in the following nearly thirty years 3,500 people were killed. Just over half the population of Northern Ireland are of Scots (mainly) or English stock, "Plantation Protestants" who have no desire to break with Britain and join the Catholic Irish of the Republic. The rest are native Irish Catholics, many of whom would prefer to be part of a united independent Ireland.

And just to muddle things even more, everybody in Ireland, North and South, is entitled to an Irish passport, and all Irish citizens have full rights of citizenship in the United Kingdom!

Although some violence still occasionally occurs, Northern Ireland has been transformed by the Good Friday Agreement, which led to the establishment of the power-sharing Northern Irish Assembly at Stormont. The agreement also recognized that people born in Northern Ireland could choose to be either British or Irish citizens. Irish citizens are treated as settled in the UK for immigration purposes and therefore do not need to obtain indefinite leave to remain or keep a permanent residence in order to apply to naturalize. Under the Common Travel Area, British and Irish citizens can move freely and reside in either jurisdiction and enjoy associated rights and privileges, including the right to work, study, and vote, as well as to access social welfare benefits and health services.

The EU and free trade have also done a lot to break down economic barriers across the border and may help dissolve other barriers as well.

What is the Good Friday Agreement?

The Good Friday Agreement of 1998 provided a three-stranded solution to the issue of governance in Northern Ireland. There is an elected Assembly and Executive, representative of both political traditions in Northern Ireland, and there are cross-border bodies to develop cooperation between both parts of the island. An East–West dimension is designed to improve relationships between Ireland and mainland Britain.

The New Assembly

The Northern Ireland Assembly has 90 seats and
was established in accordance with the Good Friday
Agreement. Members are elected by a form of
proportional representation, a vastly fairer elective
system than the old system of "gerrymandering" that
guaranteed Protestant majorities.

The Main Parties

There are ten political parties in Northern Ireland. The
Democratic Unionist Party (DUP) was founded in 1971
by the late Reverend Ian Paisley, leader of the Protestant
Unionist Party and Desmond Boal, formerly of the Ulster
Unionist Party. The DUP is currently the second largest
party in the Northern Ireland Assembly.

Sinn Féin is the largest party in the Northern Ireland
Assembly, having won the largest share of first-preference
votes and the most seats in the 2022 election, the first time
an Irish nationalist party has done so.

The moderate parties are the Green Party in Northern
Ireland and the Alliance Party of Northern Ireland, who
both try to bring Catholics and Protestants together. The
Social Democratic and Labor Party (SDLP) was founded
in 1970 by Gerry Fitt, a Catholic union leader, and John
Hume, a teacher. In 1998, Hume won the Nobel Peace
Prize and donated the money to the poor and to victims
of violence in the North.

The Good Friday Agreement was partly a result of
discussions between Gerry Adams of Sinn Féin and
John Hume, who were later joined by David Trimble of
the Ulster Unionist Party.

Northern Ireland also has representation in the British Parliament at Westminster with their eighteen constituencies, but elected Sinn Féin members do not take their seats, believing that British political institutions should not play a part in governing the people of Ireland.

Brexit

Britain's 2016 decision to leave the EU has had considerable political and economic repercussions in Ireland. The most urgent concern was the possible reestablishment of a hard border between Northern Ireland (part of the UK) and the Republic of Ireland (an EU member state). The Good Friday Agreement was built on the premise that both the UK and Ireland were EU members. When Britain left, it raised questions around the stability of the agreement and instigated conversations around Irish reunification.

In Northern Ireland, the vote exposed a significant rift between younger voters who tended to vote to Remain, while older voters were more inclined to vote Leave. Most in the Republic were of the view that no good would come of Brexit, that it would damage trade, travel, and potentially unravel the peace process.

In regard to the effect on Ireland's economy, some of those fears were realized, at least for a while: new infrastructure and customs checks on trade moving between Ireland and the UK caused massive delays and a loss of profits for businesses while the new system was being worked out. As part of the arrangement, Northern Ireland would remain in the European single market, which created regulatory divergence with the rest of the UK, complicating the all-island economy.

While efforts continue to alleviate the consequences of the referendum and uphold peace and stability on the island, Brexit remains a complex and evolving issue with profound implications for Ireland and its relationship with the broader European Union.

Covid-19

By March 2020, the global coronavirus pandemic had reached Irish shores. The response of authorities was to implement measures aimed at containing the spread of the infection, so as to ensure that the country's otherwise efficient health system would not be overwhelmed. Masks, social distancing, and hand hygiene were heavily emphasized, and several lockdowns were used at various stages of the pandemic in an attempt to keep the number of infections within a manageable threshold. In addition to stay-at-home orders, lockdowns included the closure of non-essential businesses, and travel restrictions.

As in most countries around the world, the economy took a hit, but the government did what it could to help alleviate the economic fallout; financial support was offered to businesses and individuals whose businesses were affected by the pandemic, including via wage subsidies, grants, and unemployment benefits. A Pandemic Unemployment Payment (PUP) was set up to assist employees and the self-employed who lost their jobs on or after March 13, 2020, due to the pandemic.

In response to stay-at-home orders and in the attempt to keep pupils and staff healthy, schools and businesses implemented a blend of in-person and remote learning, while many workplaces introduced remote working arrangements to minimize physical contact, something that has carried over into post-Covid daily life, with many businesses having returned to their offices, but now with a hybrid working model whereby staff may only come into the office two or three days a week.

While there were cases of defiance against lockdown measures, the vast majority of people accepted and complied with the government-imposed restrictions. Most people shared the fundamental understanding that observing the restrictions was a shared responsibility undertaken to protect the vulnerable and decrease the strain on healthcare systems. As the following chapters explore in greater detail, the Irish have a strong sense of community, and this was reflected in their response to the coronavirus outbreak. The commonly Irish fondness for social gatherings, frequently observed in pubs and community events, was put to the side for the greater good, which in itself demonstrated a shared commitment to overcoming challenges together.

By December 2020, a nationwide vaccination campaign was implemented that prioritized healthcare workers, older adults, and vulnerable populations, and vaccination centers were set up around the country to administer vaccines efficiently. The last remaining coronavirus-related measure was the mandatory wearing of masks in medical settings, but this requirement was removed in April 2023. Some individuals, often those with compromised immune systems, continue to wear masks in social settings, but it's no longer compulsory.

CHAPTER TWO

VALUES &
ATTITUDES

"We Irish prefer embroideries to plain cloth. To us Irish, memory is a canvas—stretched, primed, and ready for painting on. We love the 'story' part of the word 'history,' and we love it trimmed out with color and drama, ribbons and bows. Listen to our tunes, observe a Celtic scroll: we always decorate our essence."

Frank Delaney—Irish novelist, journalist, and broadcaster

IRISHNESS

Ireland is a nation rich in history and culture. It has vibrant traditions, fascinating folklore, and a strong sense of community. Throughout their long struggle for independence, the Irish have always maintained a pride in their heritage, which includes language, literature, religion, art, and dance.

The Ties That Bind

The Irish place significant importance on family and community. The ancient concept of *meitheal*, a co-operative system where groups of neighbors help each other with farming work, highlights the Irish spirit. While the Irish are also famous for begrudging one another, they believe in supporting their community and will lend a helping hand. Ireland has consistently been one of the most charitable countries in Europe over the last decade. Family gatherings, such as weddings, communions, and holiday celebrations, are of great priority and a large effort is always made.

Language

In Ireland both English and Irish (Gaeilge) are official languages. You will become acquainted with Irish almost as soon as you arrive, with street and road signs being written in both languages. English is the predominant language used in daily life, but with people from so many countries now calling Ireland home, you will hear a great variety of languages as you roam the streets.

Irish, sometimes referred to as Gaelic, is part of the Celtic language family and is spoken by just under 2 million people in Ireland today (about 40 percent of inhabitants), which represents an increase in speakers of around 6 percent since 2016. Of those who speak Irish, around half noted that they use it on a daily basis. The language, the written form of which dates back to the fourth century CE, is a core subject in the school curriculum and its study is compulsory. While not all achieve fluency, even those that may resent the long hours spent studying its complex grammar at school would still hate to see it disappear. It's quite common for people to use a few familiar phrases, sometimes referred to as "*Cúpla Focal*," in everyday conversation—even if it is only to wish you *sláinte* ("slawn-cha"), good health! On your travels you may sometimes see someone with a little gold harp pinned to their lapel; this is the *Fáinne* ("fawn-ya"), a symbol worn to mark that they are an Irish speaker. For more on Gaelic and its development and use today, see page 97.

Greedy of Praise?

Oliver St. John Gogarty, one of the great Irish wits (he is the inspiration for Buck Mulligan in Joyce's *Ulysses*), once wrote that "You should never praise one Irishman to another," and Irishmen do perhaps have a tendency to criticize each other. "Begrudgery" is something that comes naturally to the Irish. Known for being generous, when it comes to being happy for someone, they can sometimes be quite the opposite. For the most part, though, having become somewhat self-aware of the trait, begrudgery is today mostly done in good humor and locals are instead more inclined to take pride in another's success, claiming them as "one of our own."

Banter holds a special place in Irish culture. Playful teasing is an innate part of social interaction here and creates a great sense of camaraderie. Irish people are known for their quick wit, humor, and their ability to make light of any situation. You'll often hear a burst of laughter at someone's expense down the pub or around the dinner table. Those who are particularly adept at instantaneously producing an amusing retort or a subtle swipe may be said to possess "the gift of the gab." While banter is reliant on self-deprecating humor, it's worthwhile remaining mindful of cultural and individual sensitivities. That said, there's no need to take the Irish too seriously because they often don't do so themselves. Above all, the ability to be able to laugh at yourself is an essential element of Irish culture.

Folklore and Literature

The Irish have a rich tradition of storytelling and mythology which continues to play a meaningful role in their cultural life. Legends are passed down orally from generation to generation, ensuring that these tales continue to impart their wisdom and contribute to people's sense of their cultural history. One such legend recounts the story of warrior hero Cú Chulainn, who was known for his incredible strength and unfortunate destiny. Arguably the most famous event in his story is when he single-handedly defended Ulster against the armies of queen Medb of Connacht in Táin Bó Cúailnge (The Cattle Raid of Cooley). Cú Chulainn had a *geis* (similar to a curse). The *geis* was broken during battle, and in his last battle, though mortally wounded, he tied himself to a standing stone to die on his feet facing his enemies.

Ireland also boasts a prominent literary heritage and is home to many famous authors whose works have left an indelible influence on the literary world, James Joyce and Samuel Beckett just two among them. Irish poets, playwrights, and novelists have altered the course of literature with their lyrical use of language and perceptive storytelling. One such figure was Dublin-born

A portrait of James Joyce as a young man.

writer Oscar Wilde, who composed lasting works such as *The Picture of Dorian Gray* and *The Importance of Being Earnest*. Wilde's writings and plays, full of wit and raconteur, continue to delight audiences to this day (there have been at least ten film adaptations of *The Important of Being Earnest*, fourteen of *The Picture of Dorian Gray*, and seven of *The Canterville Ghost*!). Irish author Jonathan Swift is another literary giant most well-known for his satirical classic *Gulliver's Travels*. The book, originally composed in the eighteenth century, remains a part of school curricula in English classes worldwide and to date there have been no less than thirteen film adaptations of the classic story.

Religion

Throughout Ireland's history, religion has played a momentous role in shaping its social, cultural, and political landscape. Religion matters in Ireland, and though in large part it no longer receives the level of reverence that it once did, its influence is still clearly apparent. Levels of observance have dropped in recent decades and attitudes toward religion continue to soften, yet for many in Ireland religion still constitutes an important part of an individual's personal and group identity.

For many centuries Ireland was predominantly Roman Catholic and Catholicism played a part in nearly every element of Irish society and culture, including education, healthcare, and social welfare. While the Church continues to assist in providing education and healthcare, it is now with less authority than in the past.

In Ireland today, approximately 70 percent of the population belong to the Catholic Church, 4 percent are Protestant, and 2.8 percent belong to Orthodox and other Christian denominations. The fastest-growing religious group in Ireland today is those who hold no religious beliefs at all. In 2011, the number of self-declared atheists made up just 5 percent of the population. By 2022, that figure was at 14.8 percent, and it continues to grow. For more on religion in Ireland today, see Page 81.

A Passion for Politics

As we saw in the previous chapter, Ireland's democracy is based on a multiparty system that includes five major parties: Fianna Fáil, Fine Gael, Sinn Féin, the Labor

Party, and the Green Party. In short, Fianna Fáil and Fine Gael are center right parties while Sinn Féin and the Labor Party are center left. The Green Party is an environmentalist party with a focus on sustainable policies and climate action. As a result of the multiparty system, coalition governments are the norm. This form of governance essentially promotes compromise and, in a country where people take their politics seriously, goes a long way to manage political conflicts.

The predominant political issues in Ireland today include Brexit and its effects on trade and the Northern Ireland peace process/Good Friday Agreement, the housing crisis, access to healthcare services, and climate change. Citizen engagement and activism play an essential role in Irish politics and public life. Advocacy groups and grassroots movements frequently campaign on key issues and play an important role in Ireland's political discourse.

Mind you, it might take an effort to avoid becoming involved in political discussions—the Irish do love a good argument. But then they love any kind of talk, being a convivial people, and are genuinely interested in you and what you have to say.

If you've come to Ireland on vacation or on business, people will want to find out about you, your family, and what has brought you to Ireland. You could cause offense if you try to cut through these courtesies and get down to the work at hand too quickly. Like the man in the pub who suggests you should "hold your hour and have another," the Irish are no great respecters of the tyranny of the clock—if the talk is good, why not let it flow for a while?

An Irish dance ensemble perform in traditional costume including ghillie soft shoes.

Dance and Sport

The renowned Riverdance dance production gained global popularity and stimulated an interest in Irish dance in the 1990s. It grew to become a symbol of Irish identity and a point of pride when it came to promoting the country as a tourist destination. It also boosted its reputation as a hub for artistic cultivation. The show's success broke down cultural barriers and furthered a curiosity about Irish culture, music, and dance, and remains an influential piece of art that continues to attract audiences around the world. The Gaelic Athletic Association (GAA) is an Irish sporting organization that promotes and governs traditional Irish sports including hurling, camogie, and Gaelic football. Hurling and Gaelic football have gained international attraction with the Irish diaspora setting up GAA clubs across the world.

All eyes on the *sliotar* as hurlers vie to take the lead.

THE IRISH VIEW OF THE OUTSIDE WORLD

Parallel with Ireland's economic and social changes has been a remarkable change in the Irish view of the outside world. From the late 1920s onward, Ireland's chief ministers were drawn from the leaders of the struggle for independence: men like Éamon de Valera and the former IRA Chief of Staff Seán McBride, traditionalists concerned with preserving the values they had fought for. The decades after independence were marked by a sense of introversion, a desire to concentrate on domestic matters. Those who did not like it emigrated, and they did so in their millions.

In 1959 the aging de Valera was replaced by Seán Lamass, who was determined to open up the economy and cut back the loss of so many young people to

England, Australia, and America. The abandonment of
protectionism in the 1960s signaled a new approach.
By the mid-1960s emigration had halved and many
who had left had chosen to return to a country that
now seemed more progressive and full of opportunity.

From the 1960s to the 1990s, Ireland underwent
a shift from an insular and isolated economy to one
that welcomed globalization and international trade.
Membership in the EU in 1973 played a pivotal role in
opening Ireland to the global market and nurturing
strong ties with its European neighbors.

The country experienced vigorous economic growth
in the late 1990s and early 2000s that was powered by a
booming property market, a flourishing tech sector, and
greater integration with the global economy. During these
years, otherwise known as the Celtic Tiger era, Ireland
developed as a center for multinational corporations,
specifically in the field of technology, pharmaceuticals,
and finance. As Ireland was to discover, however, the
interdependence did not come without a price. The global
financial crisis of 2008 and the consequent European
debt crisis had a profound and painful effect on Ireland's
economy. The housing market crashed, as did the banking
sector, leading to a period of austerity measures, bailout
programs, and significant public debt.

Over the last decade, Ireland has continued to navigate
the challenges of globalization, economic recovery,
and shifting geopolitical dynamics. The country has
strengthened its position within the European Union
while nurturing strong connections with key international
partners, particularly the United States and the United

Kingdom. Learning the lessons of the past, Ireland's economy has diversified, with an ongoing focus on technology, pharmaceuticals, and renewable energy sectors.

Needless to say, Brexit has also profoundly impacted Ireland's relationship with the outside world. It has brought to the fore how important Ireland's ties with EU are. Meanwhile, Ireland's close economic and cultural ties with the UK have necessitated careful navigation of Brexit negotiations, particularly regarding trade, border issues, and the Good Friday Agreement.

As a small, open economy, Ireland continues to adapt to evolving global realities, persistently seeking to uphold its reputation as a dynamic and innovative nation.

Ireland Today

With an average of twenty days annual paid leave and affordable flights to mainland Europe, the Irish enjoy spending time abroad. Young people see the world as their oyster, with new graduates often spending several years working abroad, most popularly in New York, Dubai, and Australia, before sometimes returning to take jobs at home. There are also communities of Irish people living and working in mainland Europe, Asia, and Canada, and a considerable number take advantage of America's J-1 visa which affords them the opportunity to temporarily live and work there. Taking a gap year or career break to travel throughout Southeast Asia and Australia is not uncommon. Meanwhile, the majority of immigrants in Ireland come from other European countries, with a spike in the number of Ukrainians arriving as a result of the Russian invasion of Ukraine in 2022.

SEX AND MORALITY

In Ireland the conservative morals of the Catholic Church have until quite recently held powerful influence. Sexual contraceptives were only legalized in 1979, homosexuality in 1993, and divorce as late as 1995 (making it the latest country in Europe to do so). Changes, however, have continued to take place with increased public support. Ireland legalized same-sex marriage by way of a national referendum in 2015 with 62 percent voting in favor. It was the first time any country had legalized same-sex marriage by way of a popular vote. When the Marriage Act 2015 was signed into law, it afforded equal rights and protections to same-sex couples. The monumental decision signified a sea change in attitudes and demonstrated greater acceptance of LGBTQ people in Irish society. In 2018, Ireland voted by a landslide to legalize abortion, repealing the Eighth Amendment of the Irish constitution. Before the repeal, women could not receive an abortion in Ireland, even in cases where pregnancy was the result of rape or incest, or where the fetus had a fatal impairment, and so many women would end up traveling to the UK for the procedure. In 2022 a free contraception scheme was launched by the Irish Department of Health for women aged seventeen to thirty. This would have been quite inconceivable just a few decades ago.

As attitudes have liberalized, few are worried about chastity before marriage. That said, promiscuity remains rare.

Marriage and Family

Families in Ireland today are diverse, reflecting the change in norms and values. Nuclear families consisting of parents and children remain the mainstay family structure in Ireland, but single-parent families are on the rise. Blended families have become more widespread, too. Similar to other Western societies, the average age of marriage and childbearing has increased, with people choosing to focus on their education, careers, and personal development before settling down to start a family.

People are fond of children, who are accepted at social events, and if they cause any trouble in public, it causes less concern than in some other Western countries. The days of large Irish families are gone, however, with most contemporary homes having between one and two children on average. Most women will continue to work after having children, and dual income families are far more commonplace than they once were. Both parents will often work outside the home and share household responsibilities and childcare. Irish culture continues to place significance on community support, so family, friends, and neighbors can play a meaningful role in providing assistance in day-to-day family life.

CENSORSHIP

Moral censorship used to be a significant aspect of life in the Republic where a huge list of films and books were banned. A major breakthrough occurred in 1994 when the film *Priest*, about sex and scandal in the Catholic

Church, was shown publicly in Dublin. There had indeed been a number of sexual scandals within the Church. Around that time an elderly priest died in a gay sauna and two younger priests proved to be on hand to give him the last rites! More recently and much more seriously, the revelations of the sexual abuse of children by priests, and, almost worse, the way it was swept under the carpet by Irish bishops hugely undermined the respect in which the Catholic Church was held. (More on the effect this had on the Church's standing in the next chapter.)

Mind Your Language!

The Irish love talk but are no lovers of bad language. They have a rather charming habit of defusing obscene words by changing one letter—hence the often-heard adjective "fecking." James Joyce's *Ulysses*, which was banned in both England and Ireland when it was published in 1922, is famously sexually explicit. But Joyce knew his countrymen well and the only characters who actually utter the "F-word" or any other obscenities are a pair of drunken English soldiers.

Censorship is now for the most part a thing of the past, with freedom of expression and press both guaranteed in the Irish Constitution. Indeed, only one book has been banned since 1998: *The Raped Little Runaway* by Jean Martin, which was deemed "indecent or obscene." Other well-known books that were once banned include *The Country Girls* by Edna O'Brien in 1960 and *The Dark* by John McGahern in 1965. Beyond the printed word, Ireland is now grappling with the issue of online content particularly with regard to younger internet users. To tackle the dangers posed, an Online Safety and Media Regulation Act was signed into law in December 2022. In March 2023, a newly created Coimisiún na Meán (Media Commission) became Ireland's regulator for all digital content, television broadcasting, and on-demand video streaming services.

SOCIAL ATTITUDES AND THE TV SCREEN

A now-dead member of the Oireachtas (Parliament) once famously claimed there had been no sex in Ireland before television. In a sense he had a point: the developing openness about sexuality in Ireland is a by-product of television and the wider media challenging of social attitudes.

Television officially debuted in Ireland in 1961 with the launch of Teilifís Éireann, now known as RTÉ (Raidió Teilifís Éireann). The introduction of television was indeed a revolutionary event in Irish society; it brought the outside world into people's homes and connected them to events and information beyond their front door.

Irish television's legendary *The Late Late Show* has provided a forum for debating issues of Irish life for more than a generation, but even more influential has been the widespread availability of American and British television through satellite and cable, and today through online streaming services. Access to these programs have undoubtedly played a part in shaping the values of the under-forty generation, who now make up the majority of Ireland's population.

CHANGING TIMES

As we've seen, Irish society was deeply influenced by conservative Catholic values for much of its history. Recent decades have seen attitudes change quite markedly, and that trend continues, particularly for those under the age of forty. More and more are comfortable dispensing with religious dogma, and many things that were once deemed unacceptable, such as divorce, gay marriage, and abortion, are now legally protected rights in Irish society. While this may not differ greatly to the trends in other countries, what is notable is that these changes were created from the "bottom up" and by way of public referendum, rather than being enforced "from above," (or from Brussels). It was Irish public opinion that prompted these changes, not the other way round.

Diversity

Ireland has become more diverse, and the younger generation welcomes this diversity. Younger Irish people are interested in nurturing a more inclusive society and are more open to those from different cultures and backgrounds. This shift is reflected in the growing popularity of cultural festivals, multicultural events, and a growing acceptance of LGBTQ rights.

Irish society has done much to further equality between the genders, but there is still a way to go to achieve full parity, particularly when it comes to wages. Women today are more likely to hold leadership positions, however, and there is a far greater awareness of gender bias and discrimination. Movements such as #MeToo have promoted conversations around consent, harassment, and gender dynamics in the workplace, pushing for more equality.

Future Concerns

Environmental concerns have emerged as a top focus with younger people demanding more sustainable practices such as increased use of renewable energy sources. The housing crisis, with a lack of affordable housing is also an urgent concern. There have been growing demands for the government to intervene and change policies to address this crisis.

This generation appreciates education and life-long learning to stay competitive in an ever-changing job market. Gone are the days of staying in one job, or even industry, for your entire working life. The work-life balance is also more of a priority than for generations before them and flexible working arrangements over long office hours have redefined the traditional working model.

Public awareness around mental health has grown as the issue becomes less stigmatized in Irish society. In parallel, access to resources has grown. It seems likely that the progressive values of younger Irish citizens will play an increasingly central role in shaping Irish society in the future.

CHAPTER THREE

RELIGION & TRADITIONS

For all the changes discussed in the previous chapter, Ireland's Catholic tradition maintains a palpable presence; there are shrines by the roadside, parking lots around the churches built to accommodate large crowds for Mass on Sundays, and many drivers in the Republic will cross themselves if they pass a church or a shrine.

In the seventies, Sunday Mass attendance in Ireland was over 90 percent; by 2016, this figure was down to 36 percent, and has no doubt fallen further still. While Roman Catholicism remains the religion with the largest number of adherents, religious affiliations have diversified, and those who profess no religious beliefs today make up the largest-growing group.

Dublin's Christ Church, located in the city center.

THE CATHOLIC CHURCH AND
THE IRISH GOVERNMENT

Church and State in Ireland have historically been
deeply entwined. Before gaining independence from
British rule in 1922, the Church frequently acted as a
protector of Irish national identity and cultural heritage.
Following independence, the old and unquestioning faith
in the Catholic Church's moral authority was greatly
strengthened with what the new regime was to call its
"filial loyalty and devotion" to the Pope. The Constitution
of 1937 went on to recognize the exceptional role of the
Catholic Church in Irish society and granted it extensive

authority in areas such as education, healthcare, and law.

The Church's dominance, however, was delivered a mortal blow at the end of the twentieth century when it was confronted with numerous abuse scandals involving priests and other members of the religious order. The scandals exposed rampant and systemic child abuse and concealment and drove a deep loss of trust in Church leadership. The government responded by initiating several investigations (such as the Murphy Report and the Ryan Report) that exposed the extent of the corruption in the Church and its institutions. In 2011, then Taoiseach Enda Kenny spoke in the Dail of the "dysfunction, disconnection, elitism … the narcissism that dominate the culture of the Vatican." He went on, "The delinquency and arrogance of a particular version … of 'morality' … will no longer be tolerated or ignored …. Today, that Church needs to be a penitent Church, a Church truly and deeply penitent for the horrors it perpetrated, hid, and denied."

NEW ATTITUDES

Even before these scandals came to light Irish men and women had become less willing to accept unquestioningly the Church's teachings on such matters as contraception. But in 2015 came the most indisputable proof that they were no longer in thrall to the Catholic Church. A nationwide referendum came down overwhelmingly in favor of gay marriage, in direct disobedience to the Church's teaching. Afterward

Diarmuid Martin, then Archbishop of Dublin, remarked "the Church needs to do a reality check." No longer is the word of the priest law, but what he has to say still matters. Mass continues to be a key if less commonly attended feature, as is confession, and priests still perform funeral and marriage rites that are considered integral to people's ceremonies. There are also other aspects of the priesthood that people may be less familiar with: school chaplaincy, helping people prepare for marriage, and visiting those in prison, for example.

It's important to note that overall, the change in attitudes toward the Church is much more prevalent in the towns and cities than in Ireland's rural areas. For example, in 2022, only half of Dublin's inhabitants identified as Catholic, while in the rural counties of Mayo, Tipperary, Offaly, Roscommon, and Galway County, around 80 percent still identify as Catholic. Country-wide, Ireland still has one of the highest percentages of regular churchgoers in Western Europe.

NORTHERN IRELAND

The most recent Census in Northern Ireland (2021) reported that 45.7 percent of the population identified as Catholic and 43.5 percent as Protestant, or other Christian, with only 1.5 percent from other non-Christian religions. In general, Protestants and Catholics in the North are equally devout, with 46 percent of Catholics and 46 percent Protestants attending weekly service. During the "Troubles," both sides were largely defined by their

religion: for better or worse, the separate identities of
Republicans and the Loyalists in the Province still seem
to be bound in with where their citizens pray on Sundays.
There are other religious communities, too, including small
Muslim, Hindu, Sikh, Buddhist, and Jewish communities.

THE CHURCH OF IRELAND

The Church of Ireland is an independent Anglican church
and is the largest Protestant nomination in the Republic of
Ireland and Northern Ireland. When the English monarch
Henry VIII broke with Rome and established the Church
of England, he soon after became the head of Church
of Ireland when the Irish Parliament passed a series of
acts that ended the authority of the Pope. At first, many
bishops and most of the clergy refused to follow. The new
Church of Ireland, however, was able to retain possession
of diocesan buildings and lands because under the feudal
system, it belonged to the Crown.

Even though there were political and economic benefits
of membership in the new Church, a considerable majority
of the Irish remained loyal to the Church of Rome. Over
time, additional bishops and clergy acquiesced, perhaps
since the Celtic Irish Church had only surrendered its
autonomy to Rome in the twelfth century. But in the reign
of his daughter Elizabeth I, the first English Protestant
prayer book was published, and in 1550 Ireland got its
first printing press to print it. It was then that the troubles
began. The Church split between those who stayed with
the Latin Mass and were increasingly papist in sympathy,

and those—mostly the ruling classes—who adopted the Anglican rite. In brief, the Catholics got the vast bulk of the people, but the Anglicans got the churches and cathedrals, and so the tradition of outdoor Masses for Catholics began.

Once the Irish forces supporting the Catholic King James II were beaten in 1690, the English rulers cracked down and penal laws were brought in to suppress both Catholics and Presbyterians in the North. Catholic bishops and archbishops were not permitted until the Catholic Emancipation Act of 1829.

ECUMENISM

Relations between the two denominations in Ireland have been largely cordial since Independence in 1921. Both primates are based in Armagh in the North, and they liaise closely, appearing on television together to display solidarity in the face of sectarian antagonisms. Each diocese has an ecumenical director who is a member of the Catholic Bishops' Advisory Committee, whose aim is to promote unity among the world's Churches. The first ecumenical director was appointed in 1968. The last four decades have seen considerable progress in ecumenical activity in Ireland, most notably in increased cooperation among Christians of different communions working together for charity and other social services.

Since then, there have been two sets of bishops across Ireland: the Roman Catholic and the Anglican. And as neither Church recognizes the border between the Republic and Northern Ireland, both have dioceses that straddle it.

In 2013 Pat Storey became the first female Anglican Bishop when she was appointed in the Republic. The Church of Ireland currently has about 343,000 members in Ireland and Northern Ireland. As in other denominations, the Church of Ireland has faced declining membership in recent years.

Danny Boy

A local story used to tell how the Bishop of Cork, the Most Reverend Doctor Daniel Cohalan—known affectionately as "Danny Boy"—lay in his last illness. It happened that the Protestant Bishop of Cork, a very much younger man, upped and died before the nonagenarian. A Monsignor brought the news to Danny Boy and stood around waiting for the words of spiritual consolation that he would convey to the Protestant chapter. There was a long silence. After a while, "Danny Boy" opened an eye, looked at the Monsignor and said to him: "Now he knows who's Bishop of Cork!"

THE PRESBYTERIAN CHURCH

The Presbyterian Church was brought to Northern Ireland by Scottish settlers in the seventeenth century. Like the

Church of Scotland, it has no bishops; instead, elected church members (elders) run each individual congregation. The congregations are grouped into Presbyteries, which ordain ministers. Ministers and elders represent their congregations at Presbytery and at regional Synods. Overall control is in the hands of the annual General Assembly, representing all 534 congregations in Ireland. Its chief representative is the Moderator, who only serves for a single year. As of 2024, the Presbyterian Church in Ireland has about 210,000 members, with about 96 percent of members residing in Northern Ireland.

What to Wear

Visitors will be warmly welcomed in any place of worship. It is no longer necessary to dress in one's "Sunday best" and informality is now the general rule. If in doubt, a jacket and tie for men and the equivalent for women would ensure that you are not out of place.

METHODISTS AND OTHERS

Today there are more than two hundred Methodist churches spread across the island, with around 50,000 members. The Methodist Church was recognized for having taken an active role in promoting peace during The Troubles. Baptists, Congregationalists, Unitarians, and a wide variety of other sects (mainly in the North) number at about 230,000 believers.

According to the most recent Irish Census (2022), the

number of Muslims in the Republic had grown to 81,930. The Jewish community, on the other hand, is declining in size, with only 800 Jewish Irish citizens counted in the Census. There are only two synagogues remaining in Ireland, one in Dublin and the other in Belfast. These communities are much smaller in Northern Ireland but nevertheless Belfast, like Dublin, has a mosque, a synagogue, a Sikh gurdwara, and several Hindu temples.

THE RELIGIOUS ORDERS

In Ireland there are more than one hundred and fifty religious orders: Carmelites, Fathers of the Holy Ghost, Augustinians, Capuchins, Dominicans, Marists, Oblates, Passionists, Franciscans, Jesuits, Redemptorists, and Vincentians to name just a few. The religious orders have a distinctive place in the Irish psyche, largely because so many people were educated by nuns or by the Christian Brothers, the Jesuits, and other orders.

While they continue to play a role, including in education and healthcare, their power has decreased in recent years in line with the decline in religious membership. For example, there were 9,031 nuns and sisters across Ireland at the turn of the millennium, but in the last twenty years that figure has declined to just 4,494.

IRISH SAINTS

Ireland is full of local saints, including historical personages from the early centuries of Irish Christianity, miracle workers who are said to have used their sacred power to banish monsters, cure illnesses, and provide food for the people in time of need. The best-known saints have a universal appeal and are part of the national consciousness.

St. Patrick

St. Patrick, perhaps the most famous Irish saint, is the Patron Saint and Apostle of Ireland. St. Patrick is associated with the conversion of the country to the Celtic, as opposed to the Roman, form of Christianity in the fifth century. At the age of sixteen he was carried from his home in Britain into slavery by Irish raiders and spent several years in captivity as a shepherd. During this time, St. Patrick strengthened his relationship with God and eventually converted to Christianity. It is said that he had an epiphany in which it was declared that he was to break free from captivity and return to Britain. He escaped, trained for the priesthood, and as a result of a dream calling him back to Ireland, he decided to return as a missionary.

Tradition says that St. Patrick landed in the north at Strangford Lough in 432 CE and hastened off to the seat of the High King at Tara. There he is said to have won the royal family over by performing miracles that were vastly more impressive than the magic performed by the local druids.

Band members at the St. Patrick's Day parade in Dublin.

The shamrock thus became the symbol of Ireland when St. Patrick used it to explain the concept of the Holy Trinity (that is, the Father, the Son, and the Holy Spirit) to local inhabitants. St. Patrick went on to challenge pagan beliefs, further contributing to the Christianization of Ireland.

By the time he died, probably around 460 CE, Patrick had ensured that most of Ireland was officially Christian. His last years were spent in Armagh, which is why Armagh is the seat of both the Catholic and Protestant primates. As to where he is buried, the Book of Armagh on the matter simply states, "Where his bones rest nobody knows," however, it is claimed that his body was brought to Downpatrick, County Down, and buried in the grounds of Down Cathedral.

ST. PATRICK'S DAY

St. Patrick's Day (March 17) is a Christian feast day that commemorates the death of St. Patrick. The focal point of the celebrations are the vibrant parades that take place in cities and towns across the country. The biggest parade of these occurs in Dublin and is broadcast on national television for all to enjoy. People come from all over the world to participate in the festivities, either to take part in parades or as spectators. While some of the razzmatazz that surrounds it in America has been exported to Ireland since the Republic declared it a "national festival" in the mid-nineties, don't expect green beer or the "kiss me, I'm Irish!" exuberance of the American experience. A get-together with friends or clubbing is more likely. Most Irish people get the day off work so locals will often go out the evening before (when there are less tourists in the pubs) and use St. Patrick's Day as a day to recover before going back to work.

St. Brigid

St. Brigid is arguably the most popular saint in Ireland after Patrick. As protectress of farming and livestock she has many of the attributes of the ancient earth goddess. Her feast day is significantly February 1, the Celtic pagan festival of Imbolc, marking the beginning of spring. It has rightly been said that she symbolizes the way Christianity did not replace the old Celtic tradition in Ireland but rather was superimposed on it. St Brigid's Day became an annual public holiday in 2023 and is the first Irish public holiday to be named after a woman.

Brigid is reputed to have been born in County Louth around 450 CE, where she became a nun and performed many miracles. There is a charming story that when a gold cross was stolen from her convent, she plaited rushes to make a cross that would be equally holy but otherwise worthless. According to another account she once gave away her mother's entire store of butter, but it was replenished in answer to her prayers. On the eve of her festival people still plait rushes to make crosses in her name and at one point, the Brigid's cross became one of the symbols for *RTÉ*—which is not to suggest that Irish Television is very holy but otherwise worthless.

St. Brendan

St. Brendan the Navigator was born in County Kerry around 484 CE. One of the most well-known aspects of St. Brendan's life is his remarkable voyage, frequently referred to as "The Voyage of Saint Brendan." Brendan and a group of monks embarked on a sea journey in a small *curragh* (a traditional Irish boat) in pursuit of the "Isle of the Blessed." The journey was reported to have lasted for seven years, in which they were met with various mystical islands, creatures, and threats. Some say they reached as far as Iceland and North America. Eventually, they arrived in the "Promised Land for Saints" and were welcomed but only permitted to briefly enter. Amazed by what they had observed, they returned to Ireland elated. St. Brendan's adventures and his reputation as a proficient navigator means he is the patron saint of sailors and travelers, while his spiritual lessons have made him a revered figure in Ireland.

St. Columba

St. Columba, usually known as Colmcille ("Colom-keel," Colum of the Church), was an Irish missionary credited with spreading Christianity in what is now Scotland. Colmcille was regarded a great founder of monasteries and established the monastery of Durrow (est. 548), famous for its illuminated manuscripts. After causing a battle at Cul Dreimhne in 561 CE in which three thousand are said to have died, in penance he left for Scotland where he founded another famous monastery named Iona, off the west coast of Scotland, where he allegedly warded off the Loch Ness monster with the sign of the Cross. The Iona monastery became an important center for educational and religious activities such as manuscript production, which lead to the expansion of Christianity throughout the area and aided in the preservation of ancient knowledge and culture that may otherwise have become buried in the sands of time.

PILGRIMAGE SITES

Ireland is home to many pilgrimage sites that have attracted visitors for centuries. These sites endure as places of spiritual contemplation and piety. In many places, holy wells dedicated to individual saints are visited by pilgrims on their feast days, where the faithful pray to the saint. In Synge's play *The Well of the Saints* a couple are cured of blindness at a holy well and are distressed to find they are ugly and not beautiful as they imagined they were.

On the last Sunday in July, thousands of pilgrims climb Croagh Patrick in Mayo in honor of St. Patrick, where he is said to have banished snakes from Ireland, with mass held at the summit chapel. Some pilgrims climb the mountain barefoot as an act of penance. Lough Derg, in Donegal, where St. Patrick had a vision of Purgatory, is

The Sanctuary of St. Patrick, Lough Derg.

now a site where pilgrims can participate in the traditional Lough Derg Three Day pilgrimage. This pilgrimage includes prayer, fasting (one simple meal each day), walking barefooted, and undertaking a twenty-four-hour vigil. Many of those who partake find that their pilgrimage enables them to discover hidden strengths and rediscover what really matters in their lives.

At Knock, again in Mayo, there were reports of the appearance of a heavenly apparition in 1879. It is said the apparition lasted about two hours and fifteen official witnesses gave testimony to a Commission of Enquiry in October of that year. Arguably, the bigger miracle is how a local parish priest got an enormous church (holding twenty thousand people) built there and then persuaded the authorities to build an international airport!

In April 2023, President Joe Biden became the first American leader to visit Knock Shrine.

THE IRISH WAY OF DEATH

Irish attitudes toward death are quite different from those of the English. Mourning in Ireland is public and there is no shame in showing your feelings. You would be expected to commiserate with a friend or acquaintance, in the business world or elsewhere, who has suffered a recent loss.

Funerals are an important part of everyday life: food and drink are provided and everyone drinks to the memory of the departed. In the past, the custom known as "waking the dead" was for the body to remain in the house, and hours were spent sitting round the coffin, drinking, talking, and reminiscing. James Joyce took the title of his most notoriously difficult novel, *Finnegan's Wake*, from a popular comic song about just such an event.

You will sometimes hear the expression "an American wake." In the old days when people emigrated to America there seemed little chance that they would ever see their friends and relatives again. A farewell party, with plenty of food, drink, and "*craic*" (an Irish slang term for a good time) would be had for those departing.

GAELIC: THE ANCIENT IRISH LANGUAGE

Two thousand years ago much of Western Europe spoke some form of Celtic language. Irish Gaelic is the oldest of the still-spoken Celtic tongues and its written form can be traced back to at least the fourth century CE. Like other Celtic languages—Scots Gallic, Welsh, and Breton—it has characteristics that seem strange to modern English speakers, and it explains much of how the Irish speak English today. For example, when you hear Irish people say things like "I'm after breaking a plate," or "I do be coming here often," it's because these constructions have carried over from Irish. Additionally, Irish is inflected at the start of words, not the end. So, for example, the word *bad* ("bard") means boat: "his boat" is "*a bad*," but "her boat" sounds completely different—"*a bhad*" ("vard")—and "their boat" is "*a mbad*" ("mard"), different again!

During the Middle Ages, Irish was spoken extensively and was the language of the ruling classes and the Church. That changed when the Normans invaded in the late twelfth century, at which point English became the dominant tongue of the ruling classes.

In the following centuries, the use of Irish was suppressed, particularly during the English colonization of Ireland in the 1600s. At that time, the English government implemented policies to "anglicize" the Irish population, which included banning the use of Irish in schools and government, and heavy fines were levied on those who spoke it in public.

The Gaelic alphabet was developed from the Latin script in the sixth century, and Irish is the earliest European language north of the Alps in which extensive writings exist. Prior to this, young bards were rigorously trained to commit thousands of lines to memory.

During the period that British authorities suppressed the use of Irish, the language continued to be taught in illegal "hedge schools" scattered through the countryside. In his play *Translations*, set in the early nineteenth century, Brian Friel portrays one such school. He also shows how, when the first Ordnance Survey team arrived in Ireland to map the land, it used local people to explain the Irish names, which were then anglicized into the forms used today.

The Gaelic Revival

Despite the attempts to suppress it, Irish has survived as a living language. In the late nineteenth century, there was a resurgence of interest in the Irish language, led by the Gaelic Revival movement. The movement established language schools, cultural organizations, and the creation of new literature, poetry, and theater in Irish.

Today, Irish is spoken by around 1 million people on a daily basis, many of them in the regions of western Gaeltacht, as well as by a small number of people in Northern Ireland. It is also taught in schools and universities and its proliferation supported by the Irish government. While most don't speak it fluently, far more claim some level of proficiency, including those who live in Ireland's main cities. Despite the lack of verbal fluency, most retain an attachment to the language and will pepper everyday conversation with words and phrases that they are familiar with.

Foreigners are not expected to speak or understand Irish, but the visitor who does make even a minimal effort will be viewed more favorably than those who don't try at all. All the more so if you show an awareness that the Irish language is the repository of a marvelous literary tradition.

Regional Variation

Even with a comparatively low number of fluent speakers, Irish still has several very distinct dialects. A native speaker from Connemara I once met thought Ulster Gaelic was a foreign language when he heard it on the radio! Today there are three primary dialects: Munster, Connacht, and Ulster, all of which have distinctive accents and vocabulary. It is said there is also now a new dialect developing: Urban Irish. It refers to the Irish spoken outside the Gaeltachts and most often in the cities.

MYTHOLOGY

Just as the Greeks are proud of and familiar with their mythology, so the Irish are proud of and familiar with theirs. Forming a broad and rich cannon, Irish mythology includes a collection of stories, legends, and beliefs that have all culturally and even spiritually influenced the country to some degree.

Stories that were composed three centuries before Christ were passed on by generations of bards and written down by monks from the seventh century onward. Translated into English by Lady Augusta Gregory at the beginning of the twentieth century, they inspired the works of the great Irish writers of the period, especially Synge and Yeats, and were central to Ireland's rediscovery of its identity and heritage.

At the core of Irish mythology are deities like the Tuatha Dé Danann (Tribe of the Gods), a magical race that inhabited Ireland before the arrival of humans. The concept of the Celtic otherworld, known as Tír na nÓg, is a recurring theme in Irish mythology. It is described as an island paradise and supernatural realm of everlasting youth, beauty, health, abundance, and joy. Sacred sites, such as ancient mounds in stone circles that are believed to be portals to the other world, are locations where ancient deities once lived. To this day, Irish mythology inspires literature, art, and a sense of connection to the land.

Legendary Cycles

The legends that make up Ireland's mythology have been collected into four cycles, the earliest of which is known as the Mythological Cycle. Its main text, *The Book of Invasions* (*Lebor Gabála Érenn*) is an abridged compilation on the origins of Ireland and its extraordinary deities. The original was more expansive, but is thought to have perished in Viking raids. The *Book of Invasions* tells of how Ireland was settled six times by six different groups of people: the people of the Cessair, the people of Partholón, the people of Nemed, the Fir Bolg, the Tuatha Dé Danann, and the Milesians. The book teaches that the first four groups were wiped out or forced to leave the island; the fifth group represents Ireland's pagan gods, while the final group represents the ancestors of Irish people today. As the Mythological Cycle is the most ancient of the four, it is also the least preserved.

The Ulster Cycle, perhaps the most famous cycle, originates sometime between the third and first centuries BCE and includes famous characters like Fergus, the exiled King of Ulster, and Queen Medb (Maeve), the proud, scheming queen behind the Cattle Raid of Cooley.

When Queen Medb of Connacht and her husband King Ailill compare their riches, Medb grows jealous believing her husband's fortune to be greater than hers because of his great white bull. She requests to borrow the Brown Bull of Cooley for one year in exchange for fifty cows and some land. Dáire mac Fiachna accepts but before he gives her the bull, he overhears that she had plotted to take the bull by force had he not accepted. Out of defiance he refused to give it to her and so began the Cattle Raid of Cooley (Táin Bó Cúailnge). This epic and other stories explore themes of heroism, honor, and complex relationships among warriors, rulers, and society.

Mythological Cycle

A godlike people with magic cauldrons, magic
spears, and the like, and a king with a silver hand,
displaced the Firbolgs. They were the red-haired,
green-eyed Tuatha De Danann ("TOO-ha jay
DON-awn"), who were said to have originated the
Druidic religion. They had strange powers, and
even quite recently if fishermen saw a red-haired
woman on the road they would turn back and
refuse to put to sea. But for all their magic the
Tuatha De Danann were defeated by mortal men,
the Milesians, or Gaels, "valiant, voluble, laughing
and warlike, brown-haired, bright-eyed, skilled
in the arts of peace and battle." The Tuatha De
Danann were forced to live underground, coming
out only at night. Ireland is full of Iron Age
Barrows, or tumuli, and these were assumed to be
the homes of the defeated magicians.

The Fenian Cycle was most likely composed about
300 CE and follows the adventures of the Fianna, a
legendary warrior band led by Fionn Mac Cumhaill
(Finn MacCool). Perhaps the most well-known Fenian
myth is the Salmon of Knowledge. The young Fionn
lives with his tutor Finegas, who has spent years in
search of the Salmon of Knowledge. The magical fish
is thought to contain all the wisdom of the world and
whoever consumes it is thought to gain that knowledge.
Finegas eventually catches the salmon and instructs
Fionn to cook it but on no account to eat any of it.

Fionn cooked the salmon, turning it over and over, but when he touched the fish with his thumb to see if it was cooked, his finger was burnt and so he put it in his mouth to ease the pain. When Finegas arises, he sees in Fionn's eyes that he has acquired the knowledge of the magical fish. Although he is disappointed that it was not him who acquired it, he is happy for him and encourages him to become a good leader with all of his wisdom.

Finally, the Historical Cycle includes legendary stories of real people and is heavily Christianized. The stories are more factual than supernatural and contain stories relating to kingship of the land. The Battle of Clontaf falls into this cycle and tells how the High King of Ireland Brian Boru led an army to defeat the Vikings and drive them out. Against all odds they were victorious, though he lost his life on the battlefield.

IRISH FAIRY LORE

Ireland is famous for its fairy lore, many of which are rooted in the land's pre-Christian traditions. In Irish, fairies are known as *aos sí*, meaning "people of the fairy mounds." In the Mythological Cycle it is recorded that, after the Milesians defeated the Tuatha Dé Danann, this magical race retreated from human sight beneath the ground where they became the *aos sí* and lived in Tír na nÓg (pronounced "tear-na nohg"), the Land of Perpetual Youth. So, the Tuatha Dé Danann became "the people" (never "the little people," many were pretty big) as the Irish called the fairies. The Tuatha Dé Danann may be referred to as god, gods, goddesses, or more broadly as supernatural beings. These highly resentful former rulers of the island are anything but charming.

The *bean sidhe* ("BAN-shee," or "woman of the fairies") is a female spirit that is considered to be an omen of death. She roams the countryside at night and her wailing is believed to foretell the death of anyone who heard her.

The *púca* ("POOK-ah") is a shape-shifting troublemaker who often takes the form of a dark horse with flowing mane and smoldering eyes that takes its riders—most frequently those who may have had too much to drink—on wild rides by night. In County Down, it takes the form of a goblin, in Roscommon a black goat, and in Waterford and Wexford, an eagle with a huge wingspan.

The leprechaun ("LEP-ruckh-awn") is a solitary creature who has unaccountably come to stand for all Irish fairies. At times, he is a *leath bhrogan*, a maker of brogues, a shoemaker. He has a red coat with seven buttons in each row and is usually drunk. In McAnally's 1888 account, the *leprechaun* was not in fact a professional cobbler, but running about so much, he was frequently seen mending his own shoes. This provided the perfect opportunity for a human to capture him, refusing to release him until the leprechaun gives his captor a crock of gold. Being quite a tired trope by now, leprechaun jokes are best avoided.

The *moruadh* ("merrow") wears a red cap and lives beneath the sea. Fishermen in some areas see her as a messenger of death, though several families claim Merrows among their ancestors.

Other delightful fairy-folk include the Children of Lir who for nine hundred years were doomed to live as swans

Drivers beware! Road signage in Killarney.

by daylight. It was only in the light of a full moon that they could take their human form. Their spell was said to be broken with the arrival of Christianity in Ireland. Then there is *dullahan,* also known as the Headless Horseman, who rides into towns and villages after dark. People draw their curtains after dark because if anyone were to look at him, they would be immediately blinded. He has the ability to speak only once on a journey and that is to say the name of the person whose life he wants to take. Once the *dullahan* states this name, that person's soul is called to death and there is no defying this call. Finally, there is the *leannán sídhe,* or fairy lover, who seeks the love of mortals. Refuse her and she will become your slave, accept her and you will become her slave and waste away, unless you can find someone to take your place as her lover.

CHAPTER FOUR

MAKING FRIENDS

GETTING ON WITH THE IRISH

The Irish are known for their warmth and their friendly nature and as such are most often open to meeting new people. While there is a magic about Ireland, it is important to remember that life, most of the time, is as ordinary here as anywhere else. Young Irish people are as likely to have been to university as anyone else in the English-speaking world, and these days they are more likely to work on a computer than on a farm. Around 64 percent of the population live in towns and cities. The Irish have access to the same range of goods and services, eat the same fast food, and watch the same movies and TV as nearly everyone else does.

With all that said, the Irish are notorious for their friendliness, so if you are open to it, you will find getting to know them very enjoyable indeed. Basic things like smiling, making eye contact, and showing a genuine interest when speaking to people can go a long way towards building rapport and, with time, friendship, too. You needn't be afraid to initiate conversations, whether it is asking for a local recommendation or a casual discussion in a pub or café, as people will for the most part willingly oblige. And, if you ever find yourself stuck for a topic to get started with, you can't go wrong with Ireland's perhaps favorite daily topic: the weather.

MEETING AND GREETING

When first meeting someone in Ireland a handshake is appropriate. For any meetings after, a handshake, nod, smile, hug, or any combination of these are the norm. The continental habit of kissing ladies on the cheek is not fashionable. Personal relations are fairly informal and more in line with American or Australian norms than normal Northern European practice, which is more reserved.

The Irish are extremely friendly, but they also value their personal space. It's a good idea to maintain a suitable distance when having a conversation and refrain from being overly touchy. People prefer to be on first name terms from the beginning, including those in positions of power like college professors and doctors. Common pleasantries such as "please" and "thank you" are expected and appreciated. It's important to remember that Ireland is diverse so customs can vary between regions and people. Observing those around you will reveal how reserved or extroverted to be is appropriate.

Providing they do not stand on ceremony, visitors will be quickly drawn into a typical rapid-fire conversation spiced with humor and imagination, and they should be prepared sometimes to be the object of banter and a good ribbing.

HOME LIFE

Houses and apartments in both town and country are generally modern and well appointed. Neither the picturesque, thatched cottage nor the rambling great house is likely to be someone's home nowadays, and Dublin's remaining lovely Georgian terraces usually house prestigious offices rather than families.

Renting in Ireland is common. In fact, Ireland has among the lowest rates of home ownership in the European Union. Some of that is likely due to the housing crisis Ireland has been experiencing for a few years now; a shortage in housing stock has caused property prices to rise beyond the means of most working Irish. The crisis is most apparent in bigger cities like Dublin and Cork where many will remain living at home with their families well into their thirties in order to be able to save up and make a deposit on a home to call their own.

If you're in Ireland long term, you'll find the Irish to be both neighborly and very hospitable. That said, dropping in is no longer the norm; today it's more expected that a neighbor or friend will call ahead or schedule a time before stopping by. Should you be invited over for a meal, a bottle of wine or flowers would be an appreciated gift.

GET THE TIMING RIGHT

Something that can throw people off when visiting
Ireland is the relaxed attitude toward timekeeping.
While punctuality is appreciated in business settings
and formal events, because the Irish prize relationships
and spending quality time with one another above the
observance of rigid schedules, you will find the Irish to
be far less concerned with strict schedule keeping than
other Northern European cultures.

As a result of this attitude, people in Ireland widely
show consideration and flexibility when plans change or
unexpected delays arise, and arriving a bit late to social
gatherings is not seen as an issue. If you are invited to
someone's house for dinner, for example, you won't be
expected to arrive on the dot. Arriving about fifteen to
thirty minutes after the planned time is acceptable. And
it won't take being in Ireland long to learn that even
buses, trains, and trams generally run a few minutes
behind schedule.

The laidback approach to timekeeping is more
pronounced in rural areas, where the slower pace of life
lends itself to a more relaxed attitude.

Country Time

When a friend of mine asked when the buses came
along in a particularly rural district the answer was,
"Oh, every so often with a few gaps in between."

MEETING LOCALS

With people from so many different countries and cultures now making Ireland their home, many in Ireland have a diverse group of friends, particularly in urban areas. And, as a result of so many Irish having lived abroad at some point in their lives, they will also often have friends all over the globe. Both of these facts mean that for newcomers, making friends in Ireland is very much within grasp. After all, the Irish are known for their gift of the gab, and so striking up conversations with locals needn't be as daunting as in other places.

Though it's common for people in Ireland to remain friends with their schoolmates, people are most often just as open to new friends joining their circle. When it comes to meeting new people, joining a local sports team is great way of doing so. There is a great range of sports clubs around to get stuck into; why not try your hand at traditional sports such as Gaelic football or hurling? Apart from the health benefits, you are also more than likely to make a few new friends.

Beyond sports, there is a festival or fair to be found for nearly every hobby or interest. Big events include The Galway Races, Cork Jazz Festival, and the Rose of Tralee, and bring together people from all over Ireland and are a great opportunity to meet new people. Volunteering is another effective option for forming new relationships and allows you to give back to the community in a meaningful way.

If you're in Ireland for work, an easy way to break the ice at work is simply to make the effort to chat with coworkers and later ask if they want to grab lunch. It's also worth checking if your company has a social committee or any events planned where you will have the opportunity of meeting people outside of your department in a relaxed setting.

A FEW POINTS OF ETIQUETTE

While the Irish are not sticklers for time, arriving late (i.e. more than fifteen minutes) when meeting out somewhere without a valid reason is considered impolite.

When drinking, it's customary for each person to buy a round of drinks for their group at some point. Likewise, if someone buys you a drink, reciprocate at some point during the evening. When out drinking, you'll find that toasting with drinks is common. (It's a good idea to pace yourself!)

When eating out, some restaurants allow checks (ask for "the bill" in Ireland) to be split while others do not. If this is the case, you can offer to pay and get the money back from the group or pay your portion of the check to the person paying.

If you are invited to a meal in someone's home, wait until everyone's seated and the host begins eating before starting your meal.

If someone gives you a ride in their car, it's common to contribute toward fuel cost.

If you're learning a new language or you are willing to help others practice your native language, language exchange groups can also be an excellent way to meet people. If you are learning Irish (and of course you should be!), head to a Pop-Up Gaeltacht, an informal gathering of Irish speakers of mixed abilities.

TIPPING

Typically, gratuity is added to parties of six more in restaurants.

There is not a strong tipping culture in Ireland. Irish people tend to tip in more upscale restaurants and for personal services such as hair and nails. In general, a 10 percent tip is more than acceptable but all tips are at your discretion. If you are going to tip, it is preferable to do so in cash, if possible. Most restaurants and cafes accept cards and cash but prefer card payment. There are a few places that are card only but this is generally well displayed in the establishment so patrons know in advance.

DATING IN IRELAND

As we've seen, the Irish are friendly and are known for being good conversationalists that value wit, sarcasm, and dry humor. For those interested, this can make for enjoyable dating experiences.

In general, there is a fairly casual approach toward dating in Ireland, but traditional values and the desire for long-term, committed relationships remain. Many Irish couples meet while attending college and date for a number of years before becoming engaged. People otherwise usually meet through mutual friends or as has become more common in recent years, via online dating apps such as the internationally popular Tinder, Bumble, and Hinge.

Not being ones for pomp or circumstance, there are no strict dating customs, and a typical date is likely to include going for a meal, a coffee, or a casual drink. In general, attitudes are more relaxed than in the United States whereby you won't see many couples become engaged after only one or two years of dating. There is little rush to "settle down," and you will meet couples who have been together for a decade before choosing to get engaged.

SOCIALIZING

Socializing is fundamental to life in Ireland. The people are enthusiastic about their friendships and their outgoing disposition makes for entertaining get-togethers.

It doesn't take long to discover that pubs are the venue for much of the social life here and for that reason they cater to people of all ages. People meet in pubs to spend time with friends, enjoy the music and their favorite drinks, and generally to have fun among friends. Cuisine in Ireland has evolved, and many are keen to try new culinary experiences, too. As such, eating out with friends is a popular way of socializing today.

Ireland's landscapes offer plenty of opportunities for outdoor adventures that groups of friends will often take part in, whether it be hiking, horseback riding, or sports like Gaelic football, soccer, and rugby. Ireland holds a wide variety of festivals and events that many participate in with great enthusiasm. From Bloomsday celebrations to music festivals like Electric Picnic and cultural events like the Cork Jazz Festival, there is almost always something to enjoy and take part in. They all provide great opportunities to meet like-minded people, and with the Irish generally being so easy to get along with, forming friendships is easier than you might have otherwise thought.

CHAPTER FIVE

CULTURAL LIFE

MUSIC, SONG, AND DANCE

The Irish love to dance, and Irish dance is profoundly ingrained in their culture and history. Now, thanks to *Riverdance* and *Lord of the Dance*, it has traveled the world, but as to where it all started that, as with much else in Ireland, is shrouded in the mists of myth. Certainly, step dancing, as it's otherwise known, was well established by the sixteenth century, when beautiful and beautifully dressed Galway girls dancing jigs impressed Sir Philip Sidney. From social gatherings to competitive events, it remains an active part of Irish life.

Step dancing is an enchanting and rhythmic type of dance that is set apart by its elaborate footwork, rigid movements, and distinct costumes—and it's easy to show off if you know what you are doing! The dance is renowned for its extraordinary costumes, which developed in competitions between dancing masters in

Dancers in traditional costumes adorned with Celtic motifs.

the eighteenth century. These competitions still go
on today. Female dancers don themselves in dresses
that frequently include flamboyant colors, extravagant
embroidery, and Celtic-influenced designs. There are two
types of shoes worn in step dancing: hard or soft. Hard
shoes are similar to that of a tap shoe in that they create
sound when dancing. (The sound is created by a fiber
glass tip at the front of the shoe and a hard heel.) The
trick is to dance on one spot—you are supposed to be
able to "dance on a plate," keeping your legs together, your
hands to your sides, your face expressionless, and make as
much noise as possible, with the immensely complicated
footwork striking the floor known as "battering."

A *céilí* ("KAY-lee") is a social gathering involving
entertainment. Historically, it would have involved poetry,
storytelling, and singing, but nowadays includes music

and dancing. The name originates from the Old Irish term *céle* meaning companion, which became *ceilidh* or *céilí*, meaning "visit." *Céilí* dancers dance on their toes, extending legs and feet, rather than battering the floor with them. A *céilí* can be performed with as little as two people, or in larger groups.

A "set dance" is a form of communal dancing that has been popular in Ireland for over one hundred and fifty years. Sets are danced by four couples in a square, and usually consist of three to six figures with a short pause between each. The dance is derived from French Quadrilles, brought to Ireland in the nineteenth century. Irish dancers modified the figures to their own music and steps to form dances. Unlike square dancing, set dances do not require a caller: the sequence of figures is determined by the set name.

A *feis* is a traditional Gaelic arts and culture festival, though the term is now regularly used to refer to Irish dance competitions. In ancient Ireland, communities placed massive importance on local festivals as they were an opportunity to come together in dance, music, and theater. Today, *feiseanna* (the plural form), are held all over the world including Australia, the United States, and other parts of Europe and are often the best place to see Irish dancing. *Feiseanna* in modern times are generally centered on Irish dancing and the ornate costumes that dancers wear. Girls wear ornamental dresses with long sleeves and a short skirt that often feature hand embroidered Celtic motifs. They normally wear their hair tightly curled, or in a wig. Boys typically wear a dress shirt, tie, and/or waistcoat and dress trousers.

TRADITIONAL MUSIC

Dance needs music, and much Irish traditional instrumental music has its origins in the dance—in jigs, reels, hornpipes, and such. If dance seems to have become a little institutionalized, music remains vastly more informal. In pubs all over Ireland, but especially in the west, you can hear players of exceptionally high standard. In essence, the tradition of Irish music and song is oral rather than written—it is passed on from player to player, singer to singer.

Irish music has been called "a living popular tradition," so much so that people forget who wrote which song. Indeed, the long tradition of anonymous songs stretches back into the past, or at least into the eighteenth and nineteenth centuries. Tunes are adapted, frills are added, meters change, and alternative versions of the words proliferate.

Musicians of all ages play together at a local pub.

A musician plays a modern Irish harp, which replaced the early Irish harp in the nineteenth century.

MUSICAL STYLES

Irish music is distinguished by its moving melodies and has a strong connection to the storytelling that often accompanied it. Instruments like the Irish harp, fiddle, tin whistle, flute, *bodhrán* (drum), accordion, and uilleann pipes create a unique sound to Ireland's music. Perhaps the best known of these, the Irish harp, has long been a national symbol (and even achieved the accolade of being adopted by Guinness as their trademark). Both the harp and the *uilleann* ("ILL-in") pipes, which are worked by bellows and have a quieter, more mellow sound than Scottish pipes, were originally aristocratic instruments—the pipes were far too expensive for the ordinary laborer.

For ordinary folk the most popular instruments were the fiddle (or violin) and various forms of accordion

A traditional *bodhrán* drum.

and concertina. Nowadays guitars are popular, as are
mandolins and banjos, which were brought over from
America.

Wind instruments include the old wooden flute
and the humble tin whistle (a simple metal tube with
six holes and a mouthpiece like a recorder), which in
the hands of accomplished artists like Muireann Nic
Amhlaoibh can achieve an amazing virtuosity.

The two uniquely Irish percussion instruments are
the *bodhrán* ("bow-rahn") and the Lambeg drum. The
bodhrán is a round frame with a goatskin stretched over
it, played with a double-ended baton that produces a
stirring rapid rattle. The Lambeg is uniquely associated
with Northern Protestants. It is a huge drum weighing
33 pounds (15 kg) that is carried in Orange Order
processions which can sometimes be heard for miles.

Marching bands are indeed a characteristic of
the North, and both the Protestant and Catholic

communities have bands that accompany their parades and processions.

But there were also the showbands that flourished from the fifties to the early seventies and had nothing to do with traditional instruments, tunes, or politics. These were touring dance bands playing cover versions of rock and roll, standard dance numbers, Dixieland jazz, and Country and Western. Today Irish music is a rich mix of many influences, often combining traditional and modern forms. It has become international in the hands of world-class pop performers like Van Morrison, U2, Snow Patrol, the late Sinéad O'Connor, and Hozier.

Music Takes Sides

The divide between the two sides in Northern Ireland has long been reflected in their music and songs. One of the best-known Northern Irish Protestant songs tells the story of the "Ould Orange Flute," whose owner converted to Catholicism. His flute refused to play anything but Protestant music until in the end it was burned at the stake by the priests as a heretic. Similarly, many of the traditional Irish songs that are known throughout the world and through which Irish people expressed their feelings and aspirations often have a republican theme: songs like "Down by the Glenside (The Bold Fenian Men)" or "Kevin Barry" date back to the early twentieth century and others well beyond.

LITERATURE AND THE BARDIC TRADITION

Visitors are often surprised at how interested in, and knowledgeable about, poetry and drama the people of Ireland are. Irish literature is an accepted part of normal everyday experience. It may have something to do with the role literature played in Ireland's reassertion of its own identity, or simply the Irish love of language; in old Irish society every chieftain had his bard, and the villages had *seanchaí*: traveling historians and storytellers. Indeed, the basis of the Bardic tradition was in oral storytelling.

Until the late seventeenth century Irish literature meant literature in the Irish language. Bardic schools instructed young scholars in language, literature, history, and Brehon Law, and this long tradition produced many poets, historians, and scholars. The brutal wars of the period eventually brought this world to an end. The last, and one of the greatest, of the bards was Thurlough O'Carolan (1670–1738). It was said that weddings and funerals were often delayed until he could arrive to perform.

About this time, Brian Merriman was born in Limerick. A hedge school teacher and Irish language bard, in 1780 he wrote one of the most notable of all Gaelic poems. *Midnight Court* is a fine, bawdy, anticlerical, and feminist tale in which the poet is abducted to a court presided over by the beautiful fairy queen, Aiobheal, where women arraign men for their sexual shortcomings. It is often described as the best narrative poem in Modern Irish.

Otherwise, the eighteenth century belongs to the Anglo-Irish writers, and it is surprising how many of the major English-language writers were Irishmen. Almost the only eighteenth-century playwrights whose work is still performed are George Farquhar (1678–1707), author of *The Recruiting Officer* and *The Beaux' Stratagem*, Oliver Goldsmith (1728–74), author of *She Stoops to Conquer*, and Richard Brinsley Sheridan (1751–1816), who wrote *The Rivals*, *The School for Scandal*, and *The Critic*. All three were Irish Protestants, and Farquhar and Goldsmith were educated at the Protestant Trinity College, Dublin.

So, too, was the satirist Jonathan Swift (1667–1747), Dean of St. Patrick's Cathedral, author of *Gulliver's Travels* (1726), and probably the most famous prose writer of the period. Maria Edgeworth (1767–1849) was one of the first women novelists, and her *Castle Rackrent* was an attack on the Irish landlord class to which she belonged. Inevitably, most of these writers went to England to make their mark.

If Irish Protestant playwrights enlivened the eighteenth-century stage, so they did that of the late nineteenth and early twentieth centuries. Oscar Wilde (1854–1900) was the son of a Dublin surgeon and attended Trinity College before going to Oxford: *The Importance of Being*

Oscar Wilde.

Earnest is arguably the finest English comedy of manners ever written—it is certainly the most successful. George Bernard Shaw (1856–1950) was brought up in the affluent area of Dalkey in south Dublin. The son of a drunken wastrel father, he left school at fifteen to work for an estate agent. At twenty he fled with his mother to England, where he wrote a string of dramas for the stage, most of which are still frequently performed. In 1925 he won the Nobel Prize for Literature.

The Gaelic League

However, while Wilde and Shaw were making their names in England, great things were happening in Ireland. With the foundation of the Gaelic League (Conradh na Gaeilge) in 1893, intended to assert the Irishness of the people, came an enthusiasm not just for the Irish language but for Irish dance, poetry and song, sports, mythology, even clothing. The Gaelic League was co-founded by Douglas Hyde and Eoin MacNeill who believed that the resurgence of the Irish language and culture was fundamental for the continuation of Ireland's identity.

It would be hard to overestimate the importance of the Gaelic League on the future of Ireland, even though it was founded by middle-class Protestant intellectuals. It truly laid the groundwork for the revival of Irish language and culture, which remain key facets of Irish identity today. In the Gaeltacht regions, the language flourished and Irish-medium education became more common. Michael Collins, as hard-headed a man of action as ever Ireland produced, called it the "greatest event . . . in the whole history of the nation," since it "did more than any other movement to restore the national pride, honor, and self-respect."

Hyde went on to become Professor of Modern Irish, a concept that could not have existed without him, at University College Dublin, and much to his own surprise, first President of the Irish Republic. MacNeill went on to establish the Irish Volunteers in 1913 and served as Minster for Education from 1922 to 1925. His genius lay in reclaiming not just Gaelic literature but the poetry of the proverbs and everyday speech of the Irish countryman.

Above all it was William Butler Yeats (1865–1939), the grandson of a Protestant clergyman, whose work inspired this Irish renaissance. In his own poetry and plays Yeats, who was awarded the Nobel Prize for Literature in 1923, drew heavily on the Irish mythological past and so made the Irish people aware and proud of the richness of their legacy.

Yeats also got together with other idealists, like Lady Augusta Gregory, the widow of an Anglo-Irish landowner, to form the Irish National Theatre Society. In 1904 they opened the Abbey Theatre in Dublin with *The Playboy of the Western World* by John Millington Synge. While Synge's background was similar to theirs, he had lived on the Aran Islands and managed to capture the speech and culture of the islanders. Managing to avoid romanticizing them, *The Playboy* caused an uproar on the first night.

Yeats and Lady Gregory belonged to the Celtic Revival, or "Celtic Twilight" as it was sometimes called, and wrote plays set in the mythological past. But the Abbey's real future lay elsewhere.

Seán O'Casey was also a Protestant, but otherwise very different from the "Celtic Twilight" group. He had worked as a laborer, was a committed socialist, and had been a member of the rebel Irish Citizens Army. His great Dublin Trilogy—*The Shadow of a Gunman, Juno and the Paycock*, and *The Plough and the Stars*—was about the Easter Rising, the Irish War of Independence, and the Civil War.

Though put on by the Abbey in the 1920s when wounds were still raw, they pulled no punches in condemning the men of violence on both sides and speaking out for compassion. The plays are full of humor, but their message is the stuff of tragedy. *Juno* was hissed at when it was first performed, and there was a full-scale riot when *The Plough and the Stars* dared to criticize the Easter Rising—whose banner pictured a plough and stars.

The Gate, Hilton Edwards and Micheál MacLiammóir's theater founded in 1928, staged European classics, but The Abbey continued to mount controversial plays into the 1950s, with Brendan Behan's *The Hostage*, about the IRA, of which he had been a member, and later with Tom Murphy's *The Famine* (1968). More recently it maintained its reputation for realistic, unromantic pictures of Irish life with Billy Roche's trilogy about his hometown of Wexford, and for controversy with John Breen's *Hinterland*, a thinly disguised attack on former Prime Minister Charles Haughey.

Across Ireland there is an enthusiasm for theater with numerous drama festivals and local groups: John B. Keane lived in the little town of Listowel in County Kerry; his plays, such as *Big Maggie*, which went to Broadway, and *The Field*, which became a major film, were premiered by an amateur group in Cork.

IRISH NOVELISTS

Of the hundreds of Irish novelists there is room to mention only a few. Edna O'Brien's *Country Girls* trilogy draws on her experience of being brought up in an "enclosed, fervid, and bigoted" village and educated in a convent. John McGahern has been recognized as a major figure, though his novel *The Dark* was banned in Ireland for its unflattering picture of the priesthood. The hugely popular Maeve Binchy was equally at home writing about village life and about young Irish women in London, while Roddy Doyle's novels about life on a Dublin housing estate combine popular appeal with a more serious analysis of Irish society.

Flann O'Brien wrote equally well in English and Irish. His comic English-language masterpieces, *At Swim-Two-Birds* and *The Third Policeman*, were written under O'Brien, while an Irish-language novel, *An Béal Bocht*, was written under the pseudonym Myles na Gopaleen. It is widely regarded as one of the greatest Irish-language novels of the twentieth century.

Ulysses, published in 1922 by James Joyce, may well be one of the most influential novels ever to have been written. Every chapter is in a different style as, in imitation of the travels of Odysseus in Homer's *Odyssey*, it traces the travels of Leopold Bloom around Dublin on a single day in 1904.

Samuel Beckett worked with Joyce, and his plays, of which the most famous is *Waiting for Godot*, have had the same profound effect on theatrical writing across the world as Joyce has had on prose.

Distinguished contemporary writers include Colm Tóibín, Claire Keegan, and Colum McCann. Sally Rooney has garnered critical acclaim in recent years and is regarded as one of the foremost millennial writers. She has published three novels to date: *Conversations with Friends*, *Normal People*, and *Beautiful World, Where Are You*, the first two of which have since been adapted into popular miniseries. Other popular prizewinning authors include John Boyne, Cecelia Ahern, and Maggie O'Farrell.

The Northern Renaissance

The Milesians, having conquered the Tuatha Dé Danann, sent a harpist south and a bard to the north. It is for this reason that to this day it's sometimes claimed the musicians hail from the South and the poets and writers from the North.

There was the poet Louis MacNeice, then in the sixties a galaxy of talent emerged, including the novelist Maurice Leitch and the playwright Brian Friel, held by many to be among the greatest living dramatists, and the poets Michael Longley, Derek Mahon, and Seamus Heaney. The son of a small farmer, Heaney was Boylston Professor of Rhetoric and Poetry at Harvard and Professor of Poetry at Oxford; in 1995 he was awarded the Nobel Prize for Literature. He died in 2013.

These were followed by a second wave of younger writers, the poets Tom Paulin, Ciaran Carson, and Paul Muldoon, and the playwrights, Stewart Parker, Ann Devlin, and Gary Mitchell.

FILM

The 1990s saw a series of films about Ireland produced, starting with *The Field* in 1991. Many had themes based on The Troubles: films like *In the Name of the Father* with Daniel Day-Lewis, *Patriot Games*, with Harrison Ford, *Some Mother's Son*, and *Cal* with Helen Mirren. Others were simply about life in Ireland, like Roddy Doyle's 'Barrytown Trilogy' with *The Commitments*, *The Snapper*, and *The Van*.

In recent years, there has been a further spate of films around The Troubles in the North: *Belfast*, *'71*, *Bloody Sunday*, *Trapped*, *Fifty Dead Men Walking*, *Five Minutes of Heaven*, and *Hunger* just to name a few. Many of these films were not actually Irish productions, but British-Irish brothers John Michael McDonagh and Martin McDonagh have written and directed Irish films such as *The Guard*, *Calvary*, and *The Banshees of Inisherin*.

The internationally popular TV series *Derry Girls* has been praised for its accurate representation of Northern Irish culture, and its accessible and often humorous retelling of the complexities of life during The Troubles. The show, set in 1990s Derry, follows the lives of a group of teenage friends and one of the girl's English cousins as they navigate the otherwise mundane challenges of youth against a backdrop of sectarian tension and social disruption. The show succeeds in providing a relatable and entertaining representation of life for people during this difficult period of Northern Ireland's history. *Derry Girls* is also notable because for many viewers, particularly those outside Ireland and the United Kingdom, it served as an introduction to The Troubles and the historical context surrounding the period.

FESTIVALS

Poetry in Irish and English, drama, jazz, film, dance, and traditional music are all good excuses for a festival or *feis* ("FESH") or *fleadh cheoil,* a music festival, and Ireland has an awful lot of festivals! Here is a small selection that you may be interested to find out more about:

January Shannonside Winter Music Week, Co. Clare; Tradfest Temple Bar, Dublin; Classics Now, Dublin

February Éigse na Brídeoige, Kerry; Dublin International Film Festival, Ortús Chamber Music Festival**,** Cork

March St. Patrick's Day (17th); Limerick International Band Festival; Belfast Children's Festival

April Cúirt International Festival of Poetry and Literature, Cathedral Quarter Arts Festival, Belfast; Galway Theatre Festival; New Music Dublin

May Early Music Festival, Galway; Dublin Dance Festival; International Literature Festival Dublin; West Wicklow Chamber Music Festival

June Cork Midsummer Festival; Taste of Dublin; Beyond the Pale, Glendalough; Sea Sessions, Bundoran

July Galway International Arts Festival; Clonmel Junction Arts Festival; West Cork Literary Festive; Longitude, Dublin

August "Rose of Tralee"; Puck Fair, Killorglin; Kilkenny Arts Festival; Indiependence Music & Arts Festival, Mitchelstown; Galway Races
September Lisdoonvarna Matchmaking Festival; Dublin Fringe Festival; Electric Picnic; Stradbally Hall; Dublin Festival of History; Dingle Food Festival
October Wexford Festival Opera; Cork Jazz Festival; Belfast International Arts Festival; Bram Stoker Festival, Dublin
November Drogheda Traditional Music Weekend; Ennis Tradfest; Cork International Film Festival; Dublin Book Festival
December Winter Solstice Festival, Newgrange; Galway Christmas Market, Winterval Waterford

The Puck Fair, Ireland's oldest festival, merits special mention. It is a festival with clear pagan origins that takes place on three successive days in August, generally the 10th to the 12th, at Killorglin on the River Laune. The three days are known as Gathering Day, Fair Day, and Scattering Day. The key event, and what makes the whole thing so uniquely pre-Christian, is the crowning with flowers of a very obviously male, or puck, goat on the first day in the presence of thirty thousand celebrating spectators. Puck Fair is believed to originate in the ancient Celtic festival of Lughnasa that was held to mark the beginning of the harvest season, with a goat used to symbolize fertility.

CHAPTER SIX

TIME OUT

FOOD AND EATING OUT

Food and eating out in Ireland have evolved
considerably over the years, changing from what
was once plain and simple sustenance to a hugely
progressive culinary scene that values local produce
and traditional meals while making good use of
international ingredients and styles. Ireland is a
country full of natural resources and productive
landscapes that make it a creative and appetizing
spot for foodies.

Restaurants and Pub Food

Nothing symbolizes the transformation of Irish life
in the last thirty years more than the proliferation of
restaurants and eating establishments of all kinds,
many noted for their high quality and some for their
equally high prices.

In Dublin it's easy to sample most of the world's cuisines. Drury Street, Dawson Street, Dame Street, and Aungier Street areas are particularly rich in restaurants. Mexican, Italian, and Indian can all be found, as well as fine seafood restaurants; Chinese restaurants abound, as do chains of kebab and Middle Eastern eateries. There are even, despite the Irish fondness for meat, plenty of vegetarian and vegan restaurants.

For local dishes, Irish pubs offer good food and good value, especially at lunchtime. One of the most famous Dublin pubs is Davy Byrne's on Duke Street—famous because it appears in James Joyce's *Ulysses*. In a typically "Joycean" passage, Leopold Bloom drops into Davy Byrne's for a sandwich of gorgonzola cheese and mustard, washed down with a glass of Burgundy.

> *Mr Bloom ate his strips of sandwich, fresh clean*
> *bread, with relish of disgust, pungent mustard,*

the feety savour of green cheese. Sips of his wine
soothed his palate. Not logwood that. Tastes fuller
this weather with the chill off . . .

(James Joyce, *Ulysses*)

Incidentally, Irish pubs, like New York bars, are usually named after the proprietor. The oldest pub in Dublin is called "The Brazen Head," but such fanciful names are rare. Belfast pubs are much the same, though an exception is "The Crown," a pub so visually stunning that it is owned by the National Trust.

Continental-style cafés are becoming commonplace in towns throughout the island, contributing to the evolution of a whole new lifestyle. Most serve light food, and some serve alcohol as well.

Traditional Irish breakfasts include bacon, egg, sausage, tomatoes, mushrooms, white and black puddings (made from pig's blood, if you were wondering), soda bread or toast, and washed down with tea or coffee. If you are staying at a farmhouse, with luck, everything will be local produce. If you are

A traditional Irish breakfast with all the trimmings.

137

staying in town, local produce is brought in throughout the week so you can still experience the famous Irish provisions.

In Dublin, with the spread of health consciousness among the growing middle class, the norm is now likely to be a light breakfast with coffee, a light lunch, with the main meal in the evening.

English-style afternoon tea has never really been part of Irish life, though some hotels do serve it. In Northern Ireland, however, "High Tea," served from about 5:30 p.m. onward, is sometimes referred to as supper or dinner, and is frequently the main meal of the day. There is tea, of course, but with it comes a meal of meat or fish, bread, and vegetables. Sometimes Ulster hotels do not even serve dinner in the evening, and where they do, it can be expensive.

In the Republic, at least in the towns, you should have no trouble finding restaurants that serve evening meals, and many pubs serve them. Be warned though, these places can close quite early, and pubs in particular are often unwilling to serve food after 8:30 or 9:00 p.m. when the kitchens close and bartenders want to get down to their business of selling drinks.

For those who wanted to order a meal to their home or where they're staying, Just Eat and Deliveroo are the go-to food delivery apps.

Sundays

The Irish do not have a rigid Sabbatarian culture. As such, grocery shopping on a Sunday is not a problem. Irish games are usually played on Sundays. The explosion of fast-food restaurants means you can eat cheaply most hours of the day or night. The same is not true of Northern Ireland, however. There, pubs used to be shut on Sundays but are now open with limited hours. Large shops are only open between 1:00 and 6:00 p.m. on Sundays. Many restaurants that are open on Sunday lunchtime will still close early in the evening.

Service

Away from the fast-food outlets, service can be leisurely. That is to say, staff members may not always be as attentive as in America but can easily be flagged down with a small wave or by making eye contact. If you have a complaint, let a member of staff know and it will usually be quickly resolved. The Irish themselves commonly grumble privately but tend to suffer in silence. As previously mentioned, there is not a strong tipping culture in Ireland. If you do wish to leave a tip in hotels or restaurants, 10 to 15 percent is the norm. A service charge has been introduced by some establishments, however, but only usually for parties of six or more. If you are buying drinks at a pub, except possibly where you are seated at a table and there is a waiter, you needn't leave a tip. The practice of offering the bar staff a drink isn't widespread either.

Generous Portions, Loaves and Fishes, and of course Potatoes

The glory of Irish country food is the quality of local produce, and it is always worth sampling local specialties like Limerick ham or Galway oysters (served with buttered brown bread and Guinness).

Salmon, fresh or smoked locally, and local lamb are the other famous specialties of the west. Irish beef is generally excellent, though if you want it rare, usually only a steakhouse will oblige. Many establishments will only do medium rare as a health and safety precaution. In the winter season game and venison are also very good.

Old habits die hard and in most places no meal is complete without a serving of potatoes. Indeed, food often comes with two different forms of potato. Boiled potatoes, usually in their skins, will be served together with roasted potatoes, mashed potatoes, or even French fries. Except in the main city centers, salads can be unimaginative and disappointing—though like so much else in Ireland, tastes are rapidly changing.

Irish portions tend to be generous but are nowhere near portion sizes in America. A large drink in Ireland is more akin to a small in the United States. Generosity (in Irish *flathuil*, "FLA-hooal") is a much-admired trait in Irish life, and no offense will be taken if food is left.

Irish bread is world-famous, and best enjoyed with rich, creamy Irish butter. Soda bread is made of stone-ground wheat flour baked on a baking pan, and, instead of yeast, bicarbonate of soda and buttermilk are used. A cross is cut into the soda bread to let the fairies out. "Baps" are usually soft rolls, while a "blaa" is a soft white floury bread roll popular in Waterford. "Barmbrack" is a traditional Irish fruit cake associated with Halloween—and, of course, there is potato bread.

Freshwater fish, notably salmon and trout, have always been a valued part of the Irish menu. Seafood is an Irish specialty, especially in the west. Fine West Coast lobsters, scallops, mussels, and sole can all be found in the restaurants of Galway or exported to those of Dublin. They are generally cooked simply and are delicious.

Knives and Forks

Table manners in Ireland follow the English convention of holding the knife in the right hand and the fork in the left. The American practice of changing the fork over to the right hand to eat with after the food has been cut up is not usual.

IRISH DISHES

While Ireland isn't famous for its cuisine, traditional dishes are hearty and feature simple, locally sourced ingredients. Many chefs and restaurants in Ireland take pride in updating traditional fare in contemporary ways. Most of these dishes, it must be said, usually involve potatoes.

Shepherd's pie emerged in the 1700s when families were trying not to waste any food and remains a popular staple in the diet today. A real shepherd's pie is made of ground lamb, not beef. The meat is cooked in gravy with onions and other veggies and topped with mashed

From top to bottom: Irish stew—a hearty dish of beef, potatoes, carrots, and herbs; Dublin coddle—a sausage and bacon stew; trays of fresh oysters in Galway.

potatoes. It is a good and warming meal on a winter's day.

Boxty is a potato pancake that uses both mashed and ordinary boiled potatoes (sometimes with an egg added) fried in bacon fat.

Colcannon is mashed potato with cabbage and herbs. A simpler version called champ is mashed potato with spring onions.

Coddle, a controversial meal that you either love or hate, is a Dublin dish created to use up leftovers. It commonly consists of pork sausages, rashers (fatty back bacon), potatoes, onions, and seasoning. It shouldn't be confused with Irish stew, which is made with cheap cuts of lamb or beef, carrots, onions, potatoes and any other root vegetables available.

Bacon and cabbage is just that—and delicious if the bacon is home-cured and the cabbage not overcooked.

Being an island, Ireland has a long history of fishing, and seafood is a notable feature of the cuisine. Salmon, muscles, oysters, and Dublin Bay prawns are local favorites. Irish soda bread is sure to be served with any traditional meals, to be slathered in famous Irish butter.

Finally, to bring us on to drinks, two dishes involving Guinness. Beef in Guinness is Ireland's answer to *coq au vin*, and Guinness Cake is a rich fruitcake additionally flavored with Guinness.

DRINKING AND PUBS

The Irish pub has become a quintessential figure of Ireland, but pubs are more than just a place to have a

Ireland's oldest pub, The Brazen Head, Dublin.

drink. Historically, they were the principal meeting place for people in towns and villages, serving as a common space for all to come together. In the countryside, the pub sometimes doubles as the local grocer's shop and, with the church, can be the center of village life.

While Ireland has a long relationship with beer and whiskey, wine has become popular over the years and has been embraced as part of the popular drinking culture. Red and white wines are readily available in most pubs and there are now even wine bars and specialty wine retailers across the country. Prosecco has become extremely trendy in the last decade.

Ireland has a strong tradition of brewing beer and is famous for producing a variety of flavorsome and distinct offerings. In addition, there has been considerable growth in the craft beer movement in recent years, and bars and breweries are now easily found in cities like Dublin, Cork, and Belfast. Small breweries are usually independent, taking pleasure in sourcing local ingredients to give their beers a unique and genuinely Irish taste. While craft beer has been well received, long-established breweries such as Smithwick's and Guinness persist as some of the top performers in the industry.

Irish whiskey, or *uisce beatha* ("water of life"), holds a prominent place in Irish culture and is thought to be one of the oldest distilled spirits in Europe. Its roots are traced to the 1200s, when monks returning home from the Mediterranean brought with them the art of distilling spirits. Over the centuries, the production of whiskey on the island evolved, and in 1608, the first license to distill was granted in Bushmills on the Antrim coast, making it the oldest licensed whiskey distillery in the world.

Each Irish whiskey has a distinct taste, so people tend to order their favorite by name. Apart from Bushmills, other well-known whiskeys are John Jameson of Dublin, John Powers and Paddy of Cork, and Locke's of Kilbeggan. Tullamore Dew, which has a sweeter, smoother taste, is often drunk as an aperitif.

Then there is Irish coffee—hot, sweet, black coffee with a good measure of Irish whiskey and topped with a dollop of whipped cream. Though not exactly an ancient Irish tipple—it is said to have been invented by Joe Sheridan, a chef at Foynes Port near Limerick—it is still a luxurious ending to any meal.

Poteen

They might not admit it but some of these distillers had their origin in the illegal distilling of *poteen* ("puh-cheen"), a clear, very alcoholic spirit. In the early nineteenth century there were said to be two thousand illicit distillers in Ireland, though we're not sure who counted them. There are indeed still plenty of illegal poteen makers in the countryside, but it's not recommended that you try their wares. If you are desperate to taste poteen, the law was changed in 1997 to enable it to be brewed legally, and so legal, hygienically distilled poteen is now available in some liquor stores.

Ireland is recognized for its stouts and porters, with Guinness being the most prominent. Guinness, a stout best known for its rich, dark color and distinctive head, is synonymous with Irish beer culture. It is seen as the national drink—though in fact there are other, similar, dark beers. Beamish and Murphy's, for instance, both have devoted followings.

In Ireland you may hear Guinness called "porter" or "stout." Porter was invented not in Ireland but in London. It was a particularly cheap beer that used dark roasted barley to cover up any imperfections drifting in the glass and got its name from being popularly drunk by porters. Guinness began when Arthur Guinness signed his nine-thousand-year lease on a then unoccupied brewery site in St. James' Gate in Dublin in 1759. Arthur got his start brewing ale, and in the 1770s he began to brew a new type of English beer called porter. It was so successful that Arthur eventually gave up brewing ale, concentrating exclusively on porter—the now famous "black stuff." Later, hearing of a much-improved version that the porters at London's Covent Garden market had taken to drinking, Arthur Guinness tried his hand at this stronger, or "stout" version.

Today Guinness is enjoyed all over the world and is widely recognized by its legendary branding. The distinctly Irish symbol was chosen as the core of the Guinness identity—the harp, and trademarked in 1876. The Irish Free State adopted the same harp emblem when it separated from the United Kingdom in 1922. A little-known fact is that the State had to face the harp in the opposite direction to avoid infringement on the Guinness trademark!

The Goodness of Guinness

When the writer Brendan Behan became famous, he was taken up by the Guinness family. One day they were discussing the good works the family had done, and one of them said to the writer, "The Guinness family have done a lot for the people of Ireland." "True," said Brendan, "but that's nothing to what the people of Ireland have done for the Guinness family!"

To watch an experienced Irish barman carefully pouring a draught Guinness can be quite an experience.

Good things take time: a barman puts pints to rest before finishing the two-part pour.

If done right, it can take up to five minutes to do the two-part pour, after which it is smoothed off with a special implement that looks like ivory but is in fact plastic. You would think it was a religious ritual going back to the days of the Druids. In fact, draught Guinness was only introduced in 1959, prior to which it was only available in bottles.

One reason for the special taste of Irish stout and whiskey is the marvelous quality of Irish water, and this has been the case for many years. The water that goes into Guinness, for example, comes from the Wicklow mountains to the south. Spanish sailors from the Armada fleet who were shipwrecked on the Irish coast in 1588 are said to have so much admired the sweetness of the water that they "could not understand why the Irish should want to drink anything else!"

If you go to a pub and ask for a Guinness or a lager, you will automatically be served a pint (about half a liter)—if you want a half-pint, ask for "a glass."

As in many countries, Ireland has seen changes in the drinking habits of its residents, with many younger Irish now opting for other social activities and less alcohol-oriented pastimes. The explosion of low or non-alcoholic drink options, notably Guinness 0.0 and Heineken 0.0, also makes it easy to still enjoy the pub without alcohol.

Don't Forget to Stand Your Round
In Ireland buying rounds is a social tradition commonly observed in pubs and at social gatherings. Although the "round" system (buying a drink for all in your company) is not as prevalent as it was a generation ago, it's still an important fact of pub culture. If you have accepted a drink from an individual or as part of a round, you should reciprocate. It's important to note that the practice of buying rounds is voluntary and there is no requirement to take part. Some people may not be drinking alcohol or may choose to buy their own drinks, which is acceptable and will be respected. Similarly, if you are smoking, you should offer the packet around. Again, no comment will be passed if you decide not to, though you may come across as mildly antisocial.

Licensing laws in Ireland are broadly similar to those in England, and visiting Americans or continental Europeans might regard them as restrictive. Opening hours Monday to Thursday are 10:30 a.m. to 11:30 p.m.; Friday and Saturday, 10:30 a.m. to 12:30 at night; and Sunday, 12:30–11:00 p.m., with some bars having a late permit allowing them to remain open until 2:30 a.m. Anyone under the age of eighteen can be brought to the pub with some restrictions. Children under 15 can only be

on the premises between the hours of 10:30 a.m. and
9:00 p.m. (10:00 p.m. from May to September) and
must be supervised at all times. Some pubs do not allow
children at all, and this is generally posted in the entry.

The Irish Don't Drink—That Much!

The image of wild excess surrounding Irish pub culture is
just that: an image. Away from the rush, stress, and hurly-
burly of the major cities, the Irish are slow drinkers and
can nurse a pint, or a whiskey and water, for a very long
time. Most Irish do not as a rule drink every day, or with
their meals. And membership of the influential Catholic
temperance movement "The Pioneers" is widespread not
just in the Republic but in the North, too.

Recent figures suggest that around 11 percent of Irish
adults never drink alcohol. And while high levels of binge
drinking were reported among under-25s, 18 percent
of this age group also reported that they don't consume
alcohol at all.

A reflection of the changes in Irish society in the
last forty years is the way that Irish pubs have been
transformed from essentially male-dominated drinking
haunts to social centers where everyone is equally
welcome.

Today there is a wide variety of Irish pubs. In Dublin,
for example, there are traditional Irish music pubs; in
some rural areas Irish games may be the main topic
of conversation; and pubs so old no history buff will
want to miss them. Pub culture cannot be discussed
without mentioning the elusive concept of the *craic*. This is
pronounced "crack," but rest easy: the oft-heard phrase "the

craic is good" has nothing to do with crack cocaine! What it actually means is a bit obscure. Certainly, it involves good conversation, but it also implies having a good time when the drink, conversation, and/or music is flowing well.

Suffice it to say that an Irishman can give no higher praise than that the "*craic* was good." And Irish pubs are one of the best places to find a bit of *craic*.

SHOPPING

Irish people prefer to shop local whenever possible. Local businesses and weekly markets are a top choice, while German supermarkets Lidl and Aldi are frequented for their low prices and convenience.

Online shopping has also gained in popularity in recent years. When Covid-19 lockdowns were in place, there was not much choice but to buy online as most brick-and-mortar stores were deemed non-essential and therefore not allowed to open. Once these stores did open again, many chose to continue to shop online for convenience and a wider selection of products.

Sales in Ireland are not as big and do not happen as often as they do in America. For the most part, shoppers know they can get good deals in the Christmas and January sales, as well as Black Friday sales that have become popular in recent years despite the fact that the country does not celebrate Thanksgiving.

Irish shoppers are a fairly conscientious bunch and sustainability and ethical concerns are increasingly influencing shopping habits. "Eco-friendly" and locally sourced products are popular, and many are willing to pay a premium for them.

When it comes to payment, while many establishments still take cash, most shoppers don't use it, opting instead to pay with bank cards or via wallets on their smartphones. The only places cash-enthusiasts may run into issues are at some restaurants or cafes who only take card payments, but this is typically noted in the doorway.

THE SPORTING LIFE

With the growth of corporate entertainment in Ireland, business visitors are increasingly likely to find themselves invited to sports events since sport plays an important part in national life. A round of golf or going fishing is a good way to meet the Irish in a relaxed and informal setting.

The Irish also love watching sports. If a big international match is on, you may find the streets deserted. Similarly, many in the country will take a great interest in, and maybe bet a few euros on, high-profile horse races.

Horse Racing

Involvement in horse racing conveys high status in Ireland, and betting on the outcome is acceptable at all levels of society. Indeed, while the Irish have a love of all forms of sports, they love horses in particular. The main horse-breeding counties are Tipperary, Limerick, and Kildare, and mares from all over the world are brought to Ireland for breeding. The sector brings in almost

Jockeys race on the Wild Atlantic Way.

€2.46 billion a year—and the profits are tax-free to the bloodstock owners.

Something of the Irish people's passion for horse racing is conveyed by the fact that there are twenty-six racecourses in Ireland, almost all in the Republic, attended by more than a million people in the course of a year. The classic flat races, such as the Irish Derby in late June and early July, are held at the Curragh in County Kildare. The flat racing season is from mid-March to mid-November, but National Hunt racing (steeplechasing) over fences, which the Irish claim to have invented, takes place all year. The great classic steeplechase is the Irish Grand National on Easter Monday at Fairyhouse in County Dublin. Probably the most enjoyable event in the racing calendar is the Punchestown festival in April.

Dog Racing

Dog, or greyhound, racing is horse racing's proletarian cousin. The first official greyhound race took place in Ireland in the late 1920s, and since then it has become a familiar activity, attracting fanatics and gamblers. Ireland has seventeen greyhound racing stadiums, two of which are in the North where meetings are held at the Drumbo Park Greyhound Stadium in Lambeg, County Antrim. There is even a statue of the legendary Irish greyhound, Master McGrath, in Lurgan, County Armagh. In recent years, the sport has come under scrutiny from animal welfare organizations regarding the treatment of greyhounds. Reports of inadequate living conditions and cruelty prompted stronger regulation and management to safeguard the dogs. The Irish government created the Greyhound Racing Act 2019 and Rásaíocht Con Éireann which require there to be a range of inspections conducted under the Welfare of Greyhounds Act.

Football

Football (or soccer, as it's known in America) is one of the most popular team sports in the country and Irish teams play at a fairly good standard. Some of Ireland's biggest clubs include the Shamrock Rovers (Dublin), Dundalk F.C., Shelbourne F.C. (Dublin), and Linfield F.C. (Belfast).

However, many of the men who make up the Irish national team will play across the water in English or Scottish clubs. Irish fans also typically have an English Premier League (where the quality of play is considered highest) football team they support, with Liverpool being by far the favorite. It's estimated that up to half of

Liverpool city's population have some Irish ancestry.

In Northern Ireland, soccer is also popular but has been marred over the years by sectarian tensions. Traditionally, Protestants in the North support Glasgow Rangers while Glasgow Celtic fans are predominantly Catholic. Young players born in Northern Ireland and who may have represented Northern Ireland at youth level moving to the Republic of Ireland national teams has also been a divisive issue. In general, Nationalists will support the Republic of Ireland while Unionists prefer to support Northern Ireland.

Rugby

Rugby is sometimes seen as the game of the middle classes, but when Ireland is playing an international match, the whole country will usually be watching and cheering on the team. The Ireland national rugby union team represents the island of Ireland (both the Republic of Ireland and Northern Ireland). The team competes annually in the Six Nations Championship, which they have won four times in 2009, 2014, 2015, and 2018.

Gaelic Football and Hurling

The most popular sports in the Republic are the Irish games of Gaelic football and hurling. These can attract huge crowds—the highest recorded attendance at an All-Ireland Gaelic Football match was 90,556 in 1961.

Croke Park in Dublin is the headquarters of Gaelic games, though it is also home to international rugby matches. Croke Park has a capacity of 82,300, making it the third largest stadium in Europe. It has sixty-eight hospitality suites containing lavish corporate entertainment

Gaelic football; a full-contact sport.

facilities. Your Irish hosts are likely to be impressed, and even moved, if you show an interest in Gaelic sports since they are an essential part of the national ethos.

Hurling is the true game of the Gael and very ancient—it was played well before St. Patrick brought Christianity to Ireland and was the sport of the heroes of Irish mythology: Cúchulainn (literally the Hound of Cullen) was so named after killing a fierce guard dog by driving a hurling ball down its throat. The modern game has teams of fifteen players and is fast, skillful, and very dangerous—its original name was baire boise, or imitation warfare!—and the Irish legal system, the Brehon Laws, provided for compensation for hurling accidents, and provisions were also made for cases of deliberate injury, or even death, as a result of hurling. It is dangerous because it is played with a heavy "hurley" that looks a little like a hockey stick—though be warned: never compare it with hockey. The blade of the hurley is wide enough for a clever player to balance the ball on it. The goalposts resemble those in rugby and points are scored either by hitting the ball over the crossbar or under it. A goal is worth three points.

The revival of Gaelic sports was very much part of the nationalist movement. The Gaelic Athletic Association (GAA) is an amateur sporting association founded in 1884 by a group of Irishmen in Thurles, Tipperary. Croke Park is named after one of its Patrons, Archbishop Croke, the second Catholic Bishop of New Zealand and later Archbishop of Cashel.

Games take place on Sundays—the only free day the Irish agricultural laborer had, and a day when sports were prohibited by the British authorities.

Gaelic football resembles hurling in that it has teams of fifteen players, and the same sort of goalposts, where you can score by putting the ball either over or under the crossbar. The ball, which is round like a small soccer ball, can be either kicked or thrown, with one point for putting it over the bar and three for putting it in the net. Today the great event of the Irish sporting calendar is the All-Ireland Gaelic Football final at Croke Park when the winners are presented with the Sam Maguire cup.

There are 400 GAA clubs around the world, including in Britain, North America, the Middle East, and Asia. Across the island of Ireland there are a further 2,200 clubs. Worldwide, Gaelic football and hurling are played by around 250,000 people each. Hurling's female version, "camogie," is played by approximately 100,000 women. In camogie, players use a smaller and lighter ball and have different rules around physical contact and tackling.

The atmosphere at an intercounty match is always one of good will, and the All-Ireland Gaelic Football Final

in particular is a marvelous occasion with good *craic*.
Bands play and the president of Ireland throws in the ball.
Spectators warmly applaud good playing by each side, and
there is none of the hostility between opposing supporters
that can blight football matches.

Dress Codes

The casual visitor need not worry about attire at sports
events, but the recipients of hospitality should dress fairly
formally. A suit or sports jacket, with dress shoes such as
brogues would be appropriate for men. A cocktail dress or
dressy separates are suitable for women. A major sports
event may be tied in with a formal social occasion, such
as a ball, where a tuxedo and equivalent dress or gown for
women is likely to be a requirement. Invitees should seek
clarification on this advance.

Golf

Golf has become Ireland's single biggest sporting
holiday attraction, worth €300 million a year to the
Irish economy. Across the entire island there are 405
registered golf courses. Approximately 350 of these
are 18-hole courses with multiple 9-hole courses.
Courses vary from those where the major international
tournaments are held to a small friendly course in the
west where you may have to wave goats and sheep away
from the green.

Road Bowling

There is one sport that is unique to two areas—counties
Cork and Armagh. Irish road bowling is a game wherein

a small iron and steel cannonball called a "bowl" is hurled down a 1- to 2-mile country lane. Throws can roll 250 or even 300 yards. Similar to golf, the player with the fewest throws to the finish line wins. One theory is that the sport arrived with the Dutch soldiers when William of Orange came to Ireland in 1689. A type of bowling called Moors bowling is very popular in Holland to this day.

Other Sports

Other participation sports like tennis and badminton are well catered for. Dress codes for these sports are much the same as in Britain or the USA.

Fishing

With so much water in and around Ireland, and because Ireland's rivers and lakes are among the purest in Europe, Ireland both North and South is something of a paradise for anglers.

Fishing is a treasured and long-standing tradition on the island, owing to the country's considerable coastline, abundant rivers, lakes, and plentiful marine life. It has played an integral role in the livelihood of numerous communities and remains a popular pastime and economic activity today.

Game and coarse fishing are popular but for those interested in deep-sea fishing, charter-boat fishing is available in coastal areas. Ireland hosts fishing festivals throughout the year that attract enthusiasts from around the country and abroad. It's essential to be familiar with Ireland's fishing regulations and secure essential permits or licenses before fishing.

CHAPTER SEVEN

TRAVEL, HEALTH, & SAFETY

Compared to other parts of Europe, Ireland does not have the most advanced or robust public transportation. In Dublin there are many options to get around, but the same cannot be said once you leave the city limits. Ireland's public transportation is typically not on time so it's always best to leave early if you have an appointment or meeting that you need to be on time for.

GETTING IN

There are five international airports in Ireland (Shannon, Dublin, Cork, Kerry, Knock, and Cork) and three in Northern Ireland (Belfast City, Derry City, and Belfast International). All airports have taxis onsite for quick and easy transportation to your destination. A taxi will be the priciest option, so you may opt to take a coach or city bus. Aircoach offers express land routes from Dublin Airport to Cork, Belfast, Galway, and three routes to Dublin City Centre and onward to South Dublin and Wicklow. There are seven ports in Ireland with the two main ports being Cork and Dublin.

URBAN TRANSPORTATION

Before taking public transportation in Ireland, it's advisable to purchase a TFI (Transport for Ireland) Leap Card. The prepaid travel card is the easiest and most cost-effective way to get around and can be easily purchased at convenience stores such as a SPAR or Centra. The TFI Live app is a useful one to have as it can be used to plan your journeys.

Transport for Ireland buses in Dublin.

Dublin Bus

Dublin Bus is the main provider of short- to medium-distance bus journeys in the capital, operating over 136 routes. Normal services run from 5:00 a.m. to midnight. Dublin Bus also operates Nitelink, which offers twelve routes. The Nitelink service operates from midnight until 4:00 a.m. on Fridays and Saturday nights. To pay for these services use your Leap Card (tap when you board) or pay with exact change (coins only) as you will not get change on what you overpay.

Luas

Luas (Irish for "speed") is the tram system in Dublin. There are two main lines: the Green Line, mostly servicing the southside of town, and the Red Line, servicing the

The Luas electric tram passes in front of the historic General Post Office, Dublin.

northside. The two lines intersect in the city center. The Luas operates on a tap on/tap off system if using a Leap Card or tickets can be purchased at a kiosk at the stop. Keep an eye on your belongings as pickpockets have been known to sometimes operate on these lines.

DART

The electric rail system, DART (Dublin Area Rapid Transit), is a quick and easy way to get around Dublin. It services thirty-one stations along the coastline and in the city of Dublin. It runs along the coast of the Irish Sea from Howth in north County Dublin as far southward as Greystones, County Wicklow. DART services operate every ten minutes all day.

Taxis

Taxis are readily available in the bigger cities during the day but can be hard to come by at night, especially in

Dublin. Taxis can be booked via your phone using apps including FREENOW, Uber, and Bolt. Alternatively, you can hail one on the street, or ask your hotel to arrange one for you. On the street, you will know if a taxi is free when the light on the top of the car is lit. To hail it down, simply put your hand out and, if it's free, it will pull over to you. As of September 2022, every taxi in Ireland must accept credit and debit card payments, as well as cash. Tipping is not required but is appreciated and can be done at your discretion. Taxis in smaller towns can be difficult to come by and so in these locations it's best to ask locals for a taxi company recommendation or if there is a local driver to use.

Bikes
Bikes can be rented via the Dublin Bikes scheme by purchasing either one-day or three-day tickets. The first thirty minutes of every journey is free with your ticket. Tickets can be purchased from the Dublin Bikes website or from a Dublin Bikes station at a card terminal. The three-day ticket is a card containing an ID which you will need to enter each time you hire a bike. Be sure to keep your card with you at all times when using the bikes.

INTERCITY TRANSPORTATION

Irish Rail
Irish Rail is the operator of the national railway network of Ireland. It operates all internal InterCity, Commuter,

A passenger train leaves the city of Galway at sunset.

DART, and freight railways services. InterCity rail
passenger services operate between Dublin and Belfast,
Sligo, Ballina, Westport, Galway, Limerick, Ennis, Tralee,
Cork, and more. In addition to the DART service, which
operates between Greystones and Howth/Malahide, they
also run the commuter service in the Dublin area between
Gorey, Drogheda, and Maynooth, as well as the commuter
service to Kildare.

Bus Éireann

Bus Éireann is Ireland's national bus company that
operates town services for Cork, Galway, Limerick, and
Waterford. They also operate commuter and intercity bus
services throughout Ireland. Bus Éireann offers commuter,
rural, and local services, city and town services, airport
connect services, and a Wild Atlantic Way service that
will help to get you off the beaten track.

Car Rental

Car hire in Ireland allows for more exploration of the country, making hard-to-reach destinations more accessible. Most cars in Ireland are operated by a manual gear shift, but most car rental car companies also have automatic vehicles available. It is recommended to obtain insurance coverage from the car rental company to protect yourself against any possible damage or accidents. Keep in mind when renting a car that parking in towns is usually limited and typically requires payment.

Roads

The Irish drive on the left side of the road. Roads in rural areas are commonly narrower than in the cities. Roundabouts are prevalent and they can be disorienting if you are not familiar with them. Take your time and be observant to the flow of traffic. In Northern Ireland and Ireland, the motorway (similar to a highway) is marked with an "M." In Ireland there is a toll charge for their use which can be paid with change or by debit/credit card. Service stations are as close to a rest stop as you will get, but these are not as convenient to come by as in America. If you see a sign for one and you need to get gas (petrol) or use the bathroom, stop, because it could be miles before another is available.

WHERE TO STAY

Ireland offers an assortment of accommodation choices for different types of trips and budgets, whether you're

exploring urban centers or enjoying the countryside. Big
cities like Dublin, Cork, and Galway offer a wide range
of hotels catering to various budgets. Most hotels provide
amenities such as restaurants, bars, gyms, and conference
facilities. Travelers looking for budget-friendly options
can opt for hostels which offer dormitory style or private
rooms at a lower cost. Hostels are also a great way to
meet others on their travels. Communal spaces and
social activities are often provided in hostels.

If you'll be spending an extended amount of time
in Ireland, or prefer more space, a serviced apartment
provides a home-like experience with the convenience
of hotel services. Alternatively, property rental platform
Airbnb offers authentic stays in Irish houses and
apartments throughout the island. Connecting with locals
who run the lodgings can often make for a memorable
part of the trip and you are likely to receive good
recommendations.

HEALTH

Healthcare in Ireland is considered to be exceptional
and is available to all citizens and legal residents. Ireland
has a publicly funded healthcare system known as the
Health Service Executive (HSE), which runs all of the
country's public health services. While Ireland provides
healthcare to eligible individuals through the HSE, it
is recommended that short-term visitors have travel
health insurance to protect against any unexpected
medical costs. If you require an ambulance in Ireland, the

emergency number is 112 or 999. Emergency departments in Ireland (also called "A&E") are open 24 hours a day, 365 days a year. Ireland does not have any major health risks or local diseases that short-term visitors need be concerned about. In the case of minor health issues, a local pharmacy (referred to as a "chemist'") can be visited for over-the-counter medications and advice.

SAFETY

Ireland today is a safe and peaceful country. The 2024 Global Peace Index ranked it as the second most peaceful and the thirteenth safest country in the world. It has a relatively low crime rate compared to other European countries, and violent crime rarely occurs. The crime rate can vary depending on the area, with bigger cities generally experiencing marginally higher rates than smaller towns or rural areas. Like any capital city, Dublin's large and dense population means it has higher rates of crime than other parts of the country. As in any country, it is important to always exercise good personal safety practices when traveling, such as keeping valuables out of view and being aware of your surroundings. When using taxis make sure that they are licensed; licensed taxis will have identification and payment meters in view.

Should you need to call the police, dial 999 or 112. Both numbers connect to the emergency services including the police, ambulance services, and fire brigades. Emergency services are reliable and responsive with trained operators available around the clock.

CHAPTER EIGHT

BUSINESS BRIEFING

THE ECONOMY: IRELAND

Ireland's "Celtic Tiger" years—the economic boom years between 1995 and 2007—saw the economy experience rapid growth of an average annual rate of 9.4 percent thanks to its remarkable transition from an agriculture-based economy to one that is export-based and grounded on the technology, pharmaceuticals, and the service industries. Despite this rapid growth, what followed was a property price bubble. It burst in 2007–8 when the American and European economies went into crisis. The Irish government badly mishandled the collapse and Irish banks received a €64 billion bailout from the European Union.

By 2010, the GDP growth rate was -0.4 percent. The public balance deficit was 32.4 percent of GDP, the largest by far of any EU member state. That same year, government debt increased substantially to 96.2 percent of GDP, the fourth highest debt-GDP ratio in the EU, having been at 25 percent only three years prior. However, thanks to the combination of the EU/IMF bailout, decreased government spending, and increased taxation, Ireland was able to get back on track by the year 2014. In spite of suffering from the legacy of the crash and colossal national debt, the Irish economy today is thriving.

The United States and United Kingdom are Ireland's chief trading partners, while other major partners include EU nations Germany, France, and Belgium, in addition to China and Switzerland. The USA is Ireland's largest goods export market, followed by the UK and the EU. The Irish economy weathered the Covid-19 pandemic better than most (thanks in part to its large pharmaceuticals industry) and is proving resilient to inflation and the increase in energy prices as a result from Russia's war against Ukraine. In general, the unemployment rate is low at under 5 percent.

The Republic's GDP

Gross Domestic Product (GDP) is a measure of the size of the economy and the total economic activity in a country, and is often considered the most important indicator of how a country is doing financially. GDP figures from 2023 indicated that Ireland's economy had shrunk by 3.2 percent—the first time the economy had experienced negative growth since 2012. The sluggish performance followed two particularly strong years; Ireland's economy grew by 13.5 percent in 2021 and

The contemporary architecture of the Central Bank's Dockland campus overlooking the River Liffey, Dublin.

by 9.9 percent in 2022. The reasons for the slowdown are manifold but include the downturn in exports, made up by key sectors such as pharmaceuticals, which alone employs 2 percent of Ireland's workforce. Pharmaceutical exports make a significant contribution to the economy's performance during the pandemic years and the reduction of demand has affected overall performance. The wider sector of which it is a part, Industry, shrunk by 11 percent in 2023. Ireland's other major sectors include Information and Communication, and Public Admin, Education, and Health. While these shrunk in 2023, sectors that bucked the trend included Arts, Entertainment, Hotels, and Restaurants, which saw increased business despite increasing inflation.

Some six million foreign tourists visited Ireland in 2023. While contributing to the growth of these sectors, it had not yet recovered to pre-pandemic levels.

Economic figures released late 2024 were more positive, with GDP showing a return to growth. This was in large part thanks to the country's skilled and productive workforce, its world-class universities, and business-friendly environment.

The Economy Today

There are two distinct export sectors: the traditional, Irish-owned sector; and a newer sector mostly developed with foreign capital based on high-tech production and services.

The indigenous sector is largely based on agriculture, forestry, and fishing. Out of the 7 million hectares of land in Ireland, 5 million are dedicated to agricultural purposes. Key agricultural products include beef, dairy products, barley, potatoes, and wheat. The agri-food sector is Ireland's oldest and largest indigenous exporting sector.

The technical sector is dominated by multinational enterprises. Tech companies choose Ireland because the average return on investment is well above average, the population is educated, and there is a very competitive corporate tax rate. As a result, Ireland is one of the world's largest exporters of pharmaceuticals, medical devices, and computer-related goods and services, both hardware and software. Some of the top Foreign Direct Investment companies in Ireland include Alphabet, Amazon, Apple, Intel, Johnson & Johnson, and Meta.

THE ECONOMY: NORTHERN IRELAND

As of 2024, the service sector is the largest sector, accounting for 55 percent of all businesses in Northern Ireland. Within the service sector, business administration and support services saw the largest increase on the previous year (135 businesses, or 4.3 percent). Livestock and dairy, as in the rest of the United Kingdom, accounts for the majority of agricultural output. The main crops are potatoes (no surprises there!), barley, and wheat. Similar to Ireland, most farmers own their farms.

Businesses in the production sector fell by 1.4 percent in 2023, the first decline observed in the sector since 2013. Heavy industry tends to be based around Belfast, but Derry and some towns also have industrial areas. Machinery and equipment manufacturing, food processing, and electronics manufacturing are the chief industries; aerospace and paper- and furniture-making are also significant.

Today's generation has seen a dramatic shift in manufacturing priorities, with the decline of two formerly dominant industries: textiles and shipbuilding. Harland and Wolff in Belfast (which built the *Titanic* and in the 1940s employed over 35,000 men) was last profitable in 2015 and the following year it had an operating loss of £6 million. Service industries predominate and the public sector in particular still accounts for a much higher proportion of the workforce than elsewhere in the UK. Above all, Northern Ireland remains heavily dependent on British government subsidies, which total about a quarter of its GDP.

INTERNATIONALISM

Ireland has become an appealing country for foreign investment due to advantageous tax policies, a productive and capable workforce, and business-friendly atmosphere. These factors have led to numerous multinational corporations establishing regional headquarters and manufacturing facilities in the country. Ireland has actively embraced innovation and technology, allowing for the expansion of sectors such as information technology, software development, and biopharmaceuticals. Leveraging their EU membership, Ireland has gained access to an enormous single market, authorizing businesses to export goods and services conveniently to other member states.

Those working in Ireland will find that dealing with their Irish counterparts in the foreign-funded areas of the economy is not fundamentally different to working in other Western countries. The workforce is young, computer literate, and professional. Even in the traditional industries, where the approach might seem more relaxed, the law of the bottom line applies as ruthlessly as anywhere else, especially since all sectors of the economy have had to survive the collapse of the "Celtic Tiger."

BUSINESS ETIQUETTE

For formal meetings, Irish men and women still tend to dress in traditional business attire—being too casual can give a bad impression, as can being over familiar in manner. Office dress is also generally smart, though in some industries, such as tech and design, dress codes are more informal.

During introductions, a firm handshake and eye contact are common. It is normal to exchange a few pleasantries before getting down to business, since establishing a warm relationship is considered important. An unassuming courteousness is appreciated, though excessive politeness, especially to a boss, is frowned upon—as is excessive praise.

Aggressive sales techniques are rarely appreciated, especially in country areas. Take things slowly and allow your professional relationship to develop as your Irish counterpart comes to know and trust you. The use of first names is standard practice. Exchanging business cards is not routine, and many companies no longer use them.

WOMEN IN BUSINESS

Though women in Irish businesses have made substantial progress, they continue to encounter several challenges. For example, women have assumed a higher proportion of leadership roles in a number of industries, yet they are still inadequately represented

based on gender ratios, particularly on corporate boards.
Similar to other countries, Ireland also experiences a
gender pay gap. Attempting to balance work and family
obligations persists as a challenge for many Irish women.
In summary, although women have accomplished
meaningful progress there is still plenty more work to be
done for parity and representation.

Despite the challenges, the number of women-owned
businesses and female entrepreneurs has increased
steadily. Government initiatives, such as the Gender Pay
Gap Information Act 2021, aspire to promote transparency
and accountability concerning pay inequality between
men and women. The act introduced the legislative basis
for gender pay gap reporting in Ireland and requires
organizations to report on hourly pay differences where
they exist.

MANAGEMENT STYLE

Management styles in Ireland are exemplified by a
relationship-oriented and all-inclusive approach. Ireland
has a special combination of traditional principles and
contemporary business practices that structure the
management perspectives. In smaller businesses, the boss
is often the key decision-maker and authority figure;
but this may be masked by an atmosphere of informal
communication in which instructions are often presented
in the form of polite requests. As in the UK, there is a
tendency for decision-making to be on an "ad hoc" short-
term basis, in preference to long-term planning. While

personal management styles may differ, there are specific characteristics and attitudes that are generally recognized in Irish business settings. These include an emphasis on friendliness and building personal rapport, as well as flexibility and adaptability, particularly when working in team settings. More on these below.

MEETINGS, NEGOTIATIONS, AND COMMUNICATION

Meetings are generally welcoming, warm, and friendly. A "down-to-earth" approach is appreciated. Yet they are still often viewed as a chance for teamwork and coming together to reach an agreement. Punctuality, informality, and participation are highly valued when attending work meetings. Agendas are not inviolate, and there is a certain resistance to structure and routine. Ideas are as important as facts, so by all means be imaginative—Irish businesses embrace creativity and are always looking for new ways to approach problems and tasks. But a caveat: such daring is not always followed up. The way things are done can be regarded as just as important as getting a result.

Some Dos and Don'ts

Arrive on time for meetings. This shows respect for the time and commitments of others in the meeting. While those present will remain professional, Irish meetings can have a relaxed and friendly atmosphere. Dialogue may begin with small talk before approaching business dealings. It's important to participate in these informal conversations rather than getting straight to business.

Meetings are inclusive and colleagues are often supported in sharing their viewpoints. Straightforward conversation is appreciated, and agreements are regularly made as a group. Agendas are necessary for organizing the meeting and, hopefully, staying on track. However, they're not always followed and being flexible is important if conversation pivots in an unanticipated, but pertinent direction.

It's essential to build relationships before and during negotiations. Building trust and establishing good rapport can have a considerable effect on business outcomes. It can take time to reach an agreement and strict deadlines can be observed as futile. Flexibility in finding mutual understanding is appreciated. Being direct is welcomed, but a respectful tone is fundamental to avoid insult. Non-verbal cues such as eye contact and body language also have a role in communication and determining responses.

Don't precipitate confrontations. Be tactful: it pays to start from a position of apparent agreement and compliance. Open dissent is rare so be prepared to read between the lines; responses can be cryptic. A period of silence in conversation is likely to signal problems. Do not be fooled by any apparent dreaminess; the Irish are cunning businesspeople.

> *"The Irish are a very spiritual people, and the longer it takes you to pay them the more spiritual they become."*
>
> Conor Cruise O'Brien
> Irish intellectual and politician

There are no direct translations for "yes" and "no" in Irish Gaelic, and perhaps this is why some do not like to say "yes" or "no" outright. Be prepared for noncommittal answers ". . . maybe, perhaps . . ." It is not a good idea to force decisions, as this may damage relationships.

TEAMS AND TEAMWORK

In Irish businesses significance is placed on collaboration and teamwork. Teams are viewed as unified groups where each member's input is considered worth hearing and achievements are often recognized as a group effort. Team members are encouraged to help one another, share their expertise, and complete assignments together. Irish leadership tends to be

Colleagues in Dublin on a work break.

democratic and encourages hands-on participation. Leaders often include team members in decision-making and will usually ensure everyone has the support and resources required to succeed. As such, team members expect to be consulted and to influence the outcome. However, be wary—it is not a good idea to put pressure on people: it tends to have the reverse effect and even slow things down. When conflicts emerge, they are typically discussed candidly and constructively. Confrontation is to be avoided; adopting a courteous attitude when dealing with disagreements is more efficacious.

BUSINESS ENTERTAINING

Entertaining and socializing are very much part of business life and are generally informal in style: visitors are as likely to be invited to lunch in a pub or in the company canteen as in a restaurant. In Ireland, entertaining is a central aspect of creating and enhancing professional relationships. Lunch is usually taken between 12:00 and 1:00 p.m.

Keep conversation easy and pleasant and let business dealings come up naturally. Alcohol can be a part of Irish business socializing but it's essential to drink in moderation. Having a drink is acceptable, but drinking to excess would be viewed as unprofessional. If you wish to avoid drinking, non-alcoholic options are widely available. The ability to relax and enjoy whatever entertainment is provided is important.

Join in and treat your hosts as friends: ostentatious self-importance will be considered insulting.

You and your partner could potentially be invited to your host's home, usually at about 7:30 or 8:00 p.m. If you do receive an invitation, bringing a small present is a thoughtful gesture but is not required. If you do want to take a gift, flowers or a bottle of wine both do nicely. Dress is usually informal but not overly casual. It's normal to return hospitality. If you are invited out to a meal there is no need to bring a gift. It's customary for the host to pick up the check, but offering to pay or contribute will go down well.

Unless your host specifies casual dress, wear more formal attire for a dinner party. Some nightclubs and upmarket restaurants have dress codes and may refuse entry if you do not meet them.

Sing for your Supper

Shyness or reticence is understood, but the visitor who, when invited, can launch into a song or a ballad from their own culture will certainly be appreciated. And it will help in establishing a relaxed personal relationship with your Irish hosts that can be advantageous when it comes to business negotiations.

Appointments

Despite the famous Irish casualness about time, in the business context, being on time is crucial. If your Irish counterparts are serious about doing business with you, they will be punctual and will expect the same from you.

Typically, an appointment will be confirmed by e-mail, and possibly with a text message reminder the day before, or the day of.

BUSINESS AND SHOPPING HOURS

Most businesses in Northern Ireland and the Republic operate a forty-hour, five-day week. Business hours are typically 9:00 a.m.–5:00 p.m., Monday to Friday. Government offices hold similar hours to businesses.

Retail stores are generally open from 9:00 a.m. to 6 or 7:00 p.m. on weekdays. Larger cities may have extended hours. On the weekend, shops may not open until 10:00 a.m. or 11:00 a.m. and will usually close by 6:00 p.m. Outside of larger cities, shops may have reduced hours or not open on Sundays.

Grocery stores in Ireland usually have extended hours, some opening from 7:00 a.m., remaining open until 10:00 p.m., every day of the week. In the North, Sunday trading rules allow small shops to choose their own Sunday opening hours, but large shops may only open between 1:00 p.m. and 6:00 p.m.

There are exceptions to these hours, especially in tourist and the main urban areas where businesses may stay open later. The holiday season and special events will see some stores and businesses modify their hours, so it's worth checking online before you visit.

BANKING AND CREDIT/DEBIT CARDS

Banking hours across Ireland are usually from 10:00 a.m. to 4:00 p.m., Monday to Friday, though some remain open until 4:30 p.m. or 5:00 p.m. one evening per week. Most close at weekends and public holidays, though some bank lobbies remain open for customers to deposit checks and cash, or to withdraw money. ATM machines are easily accessible and Visa, MasterCard/Eurocard are commonly accepted at hotels, gas stations, grocery stores, and retail shops. American Express is accepted in some restaurants, bars, and shops, but not all. Diners Club, JCB, and Discover are generally not accepted. Maestro, Visa, and MasterCard debit cards are accepted by all. Contactless payments, or "tapping" is extremely popular, allowing customers to pay quickly and securely using their phones. Despite this, hard cash is still widely used and accepted, particularly in rural areas.

CHAPTER NINE

COMMUNICATING

A LOVE OF LANGUAGE

The gift of the gab is generally supposed to represent the archetypical Irishman's ability to charm, and there is some truth in the stereotype. Verbal fluency is valued in Ireland. It's what "the *craic*" is all about, and the unbroken line of outstanding Irish playwrights from the eighteenth century onward bears witness to the Irish joy in words and discourse.

THE IMPORTANCE OF UNDERSTATEMENT

While picturesque phrases and colorful images may abound, this is counterbalanced by gently ironic understatement. Somebody severely ill might be said to have a "bad dose." If someone suggests a "gargle" they mean going for a drink.

This indirectness often represents a delicate linguistic camouflage under which uncomfortable truths can be hinted at, or propositions advanced, with minimal loss of face if rejected. It is important in doing business, especially in rural areas, to be tuned in to these subtleties.

At a deeper level, beneath the general bonhomie, the Irish are reticent about exposing their innermost feelings. Not as formal as Americans in personal relationships, the Irish are nevertheless unlikely to bare their souls to anybody other than close friends or family.

Patience Pays

The Irish love of conversation means it can be a fine test of one's patience to stand in, say, a supermarket line while the checkout girl chatters to the customers ahead of you about their respective families. Look on it as good training for future hardships!

WATCH OUT FOR GOSSIP

The small size of Ireland means everybody knows (or thinks they know) everybody else's business. Gossip travels fast. The other side of the coin is that most are keen to preserve their privacy. Consequently, there often emerges a wonderful contradiction whereby, in trying to preserve their own privacy, people will happily talk about others in order to keep the limelight off themselves.

ACCENT AND IDIOM

Despite its small population, there is considerable regional variation in Ireland, in both accent and phrasing. The Dublin accent is perhaps the most recognized though also includes variations, ranging from working-class city center to the "posh" Dublin 4 accent. Many younger children and teenagers today speak with a slight American accent due to the influence of American television. The Cork accent is very distinctive, but you do not need to be familiar with it as anyone from Cork will let you know that they are from there! In rural areas you can hear accents that are more influenced by traditional Irish Gaelic pronunciation and are quite distinctive from urban accents. The harsher Northern accent can sound more like Scots, especially in Belfast City.

Beware of Stereotypes

Cheery Hollywood stereotypes who utter phrases like "top of the morning" (which nobody actually says in Ireland) can be painfully misleading. In particular, visitors who put on fake Irish accents are not appreciated. The "drunken Irish" stereotype is also misplaced (around 20 percent of Irish do not drink at all!) and is liable to cause offense. And whatever may be the case in the United States, in Ireland a *shillelagh* is not a blackthorn walking stick but a vicious cudgel sometimes kept behind bars to deal with awkward customers!

Although few Irish people speak Irish fluently, many Irish turns of phrase derive from Irish usage. Irish has a tense called "the present habitual" and you might hear something like "There does be a meeting of the board every Tuesday."

THE MEDIA

Irish Newspapers

Ireland is well provided with newspapers, which have a good mix of national and international news. The *Irish Times*, regarded as the flagship quality daily (though the *Irish Independent* has a larger circulation), is accessible online. British newspapers are available throughout Ireland from early on the day of issue.

TV and Radio

The digital terrestrial television service Saorview became the main source of broadcast television when analog transmissions ended in 2012. Ireland's publicly funded TV and radio network, RTÉ, has four national stations: RTÉ One (showing news, current affairs, and entertainment), RTÉ 2 (movies and sports), RTÉjr (children's programming), and RTÉ News (rolling news). Direct broadcast satellite service has been available since the late 1980s with the arrival of free-to-air satellite Astra and subscription service Sky Television.

Today over one quarter of the population regularly view content via streaming platforms, and so many public service broadcasters and international streaming services

A man stops to read his newspaper in the sun.

serve the Republic of Ireland and Northern Ireland. RTÉ
Player, Virgin Media Player, and TG4 Player are free
streaming services in Ireland. In Northern Ireland, BBC
iPlayer, Channel 4, and RTÉ Player International can
be accessed for free. Netflix, Disney+, and Prime Video
can all be accessed while visiting Ireland, perhaps with
different offerings than where you are coming from.
Hulu is not accessible in Europe.

RTÉ Radio broadcasts four analogue channels and
five digital channels nationwide. RTÉ Radio1 is speech
and music, RTÉ Radio 2 plays contemporary hits, RTÉ
Raidió na Gaeltachta focuses on Irish language content
and music, with the remaining channels playing a variety
of different genres.

INTERNET AND SOCIAL MEDIA

The Irish are well connected. According to DataReportal,
92 percent of the population were using the internet in
2024 for an average of six hours every day. When asked

what they principally used the internet for, 72 percent said it was to find information, 64 percent said they used it for staying in touch, while 63 percent said it was to learn how to do things. Approximately 56 percent said they used the internet mainly to watch videos, TV shows, and movies.

Ever sociable, approximately 80 percent of Irish people had some kind of social media account in 2024, the most popular platforms being Facebook, Instagram, X, and LinkedIn, though usage of each varies heavily depending on age. The one app that is equally popular among all age groups, however, is WhatsApp.

In general, teenagers and young adults are very fond of Instagram, Snapchat, and TikTok, which they use for entertainment, staying connected with friends, and sharing their daily lives through photos and videos. Facebook remains popular with adults in their mid-thirties to seventies who use it for communication, entertainment, and to stay informed about what is going on in their communities. LinkedIn is widely used for professional networking.

Wary of the information they are being exposed to online, approximately 58 percent of internet users expressed concern about discerning between what is real and what is fake on the internet.

TELEPHONE AND SIM CARDS

Telephone

The telecommunications network in Ireland is an advanced digital system that is connected by a wide-

ranging national fiberoptic network with links to the
UK, Continental Europe, and North America. 5G is
available, with coverage reaching more than 70 percent of
the population. Visiting businesspeople should have no
difficulty with laptops or cell phones.

Landlines are not as common as they once were but
are still prevalent in many businesses. Mobile phones (cell
phones) are used by all, and competitive prices have seen
more and more Irish customers forgoing landline services
at all. The largest mobile phone companies in Ireland
include Three Ireland, Vodafone, and Eir Mobile.

To dial out from Ireland use the 00 code. For example,
to dial the UK (including Northern Ireland) dial 0044 plus
the area code without the 0 in front—thus the UK number
01632 961084 should be dialed as 0044 1632 961084.
To call Ireland from any other country the code is +353
(00 353 from UK).

The Northern Ireland service is the same as that of
the rest of the UK and calls to the Republic count as
international calls.

SIMs

If you are visiting Ireland or planning to stay for
an extended time, getting a local SIM card is a cost-
effective way to stay connected. Prepaid SIM cards are
widely available in convenience stores, mobile phone
shops, and at the airport and are a good option for
tourists or short-term visitors. If you're planning on
staying in Ireland for an extended period, you may
consider signing up for a "bill pay" plan with one of
the major mobile operators. These plans usually offer

better rates and more data compared to prepaid options. Ireland has a SIM card registration system to enhance security and prevent illegal activities. As such, when purchasing a SIM card, you'll need to provide photo identification, such as a passport or driver's license.
If you're traveling within the European Union, you can use your Irish SIM card without incurring additional roaming charges in EU member countries.

CONCLUSION

The best thing that visitors to Ireland can do is relax, be themselves, and enjoy the very particular experience that is life in Ireland. Though some may try, no one can master all the subtleties of the local culture without the investment of many years, and sadly, you can't become Irish by a process of osmosis. It is our hope, however, that this book will have given you a well-rounded idea of what to expect as well as what matters to the Irish and what makes them tick. We've explored their national past, both ancient and modern, become acquainted with their values and attitudes, and learnt about their festivals and traditions. We've seen how they go about their daily lives, what they like to eat and drink, how they spend their free time.

Despite our efforts, there is no real substitute for embracing the open roads and getting to know Ireland's genuine and hospitable people on the ground and on their terms. Indeed, that is when the real discovery begins. *Sláinte agus saol fada agat*—health and long life to you!

USEFUL APPS

Travel and Transportation

Hail a ride with **FREENOW**, **Uber** or **Bolt**. When using buses, get the latest schedule and journey time info on **TFI LIVE**. Top up your TFI Leap travelcard with **Leap Top Up**. To plan a journey using public transportation information in Dublin, use **Transit**. For intercity trains, use **Irish Rail**. Rent a car by the hour using **GoCar** or **YUKÕ**. **Parking Tag** will allow you to pay for parking. Before you hit the road, check the weather forecast on **Met Éireann**. Navigate using **Waze**, **Google Maps**, or **HERE WeGo**—the latter two allow you download maps for offline use. Bikesharing options include **Bleeper**, **DublinBikes**, and **Moby**.

Food and Shopping

When it comes to ordering food for delivery, **JustEat** and **Deliveroo** are Ireland's most popular choices. **TooGoodtoGo** rescues unsold food from restaurants, bakeries, and supermarkets from going to waste and offers it for delivery or collection. If you want to go out to eat, find a restaurant with **OpenTable**. When it comes to shopping online, popular platforms locally include **Amazon**, **Dunnes**, **Very Ireland**, and **Tesco**. The local Craigslist alternative is **Adverts.ie.** When it comes to transferring money to personal or business accounts, the **Revolut** banking app is a popular local choice.

Communication and Socializing

Message your Irish friends using **WhatsApp**, which is the most widely used messaging app locally. Both **Facebook** and **Facebook Messenger** are popular for staying in touch, too. For help with Irish vocabulary and phrases, use **Google Translate** or **English Irish Translator**, both of which have text and voice functionality.

FURTHER READING

Alexander, Aimee. *The Little Book of Irishisms: Know the Irish through our Words*. Cork: Deegan Communications, 2021.

Behan, Brendan. *After the Wake*. Dublin: The O'Brien Press, 1998.

Biagini, Eugenio F. *The Cambridge Social History of Modern Ireland*. Cambridge University Press, 2017

Cahill, Thomas. *How the Irish Saved Civilization*. New York: Anchor Books, 1995.

Dwyer, T. Ryal. *Michael Collins and the Civil War*. Dublin: The Mercier Press, 2012.

Joyce, J. *Ulysses*. New York: Random House, 1934.

Kelly, John. *The Graves Are Walking: The Great Famine and the Saga of the Irish People*. London: Picador 2013.

Longley, Michael (ed.) *20th Century Irish Poems*. London: Faber, 2002.

McCourt, Malachy. *Malachy McCourt's History of Ireland*. Philadelphia: Running Press, 2008.

McGahern, John. *The Dark*. London: Faber, 1965.

_____ *That They May Face the Rising Sun*. London: Faber, 2001.

Montague, John (ed.). *The Faber Book of Irish Verse*. London: Faber, 1974.

Moody, T. W. & Martin, F. X. *The Course of Irish History*. Dublin: Mercier Press, 1994.

O'Brien, Flann. *The Third Policeman*. New York: New American Library, 1986.

_____ *At Swim-two-birds*. Penguin Modern Classics, 1939.

O'Toole, Fintan. *We Don't Know Ourselves: A Personal History of Modern Ireland*. New York: Liveright, 2023.

Synge, J. M. *The Aran Islands*. Oxford: OUP, 1990.

Vallely, Fintan. *Companion to Irish Traditional Music*. Cork: Cork University Press, 1998.

Yeats, W. B. *Poems, Selected by Seamus Heaney*. London: Faber, 2002.

INDEX